Sound and Scripture
Reflections of a Torah Reader

By Joshua Gettinger

Melton Hill Media, LLC
Oak Ridge, Tennessee 37830

www.meltonhillmedia.com

MELTON HILL
MEDIA

ISBN 9780981679341

Published by
Melton Hill Media, LLC
9119 Solway Ferry Road
Oak Ridge, TN 37830
865-803-2286

wendy@meltonhillmedia.com
www.meltonhillmedia.com

Book design by
Foursquare Consulting Group, LLC
244 E. Oklahoma Ave.
Knoxville, Tennessee 37917
865-540-1338

jlfuson@4square.ws
www.4square.ws

August 2012

To my wife and true partner, Barbara Levin
Her support and efforts have made this work possible.
Patience is reflected in her aphorism:
"If you live with a zebra, you'd better learn to like stripes."

Table of Contents

Introduction: The Making of a Torah Reader 1

Preface: What to Call the Chant and its Notes..................... 17

PART ONE AHAVAH — LOVE 21

Chapter 1   Biblical Chant — Rhythmic Speech 23

Chapter 2   "This song will be a witness..." (Deut 31)
             The Melodies of Biblical Chant 29

Chapter 3   The Origins of Torah Chant........................... 37

Chapter 4   The Workings of Chant 47

PART TWO: YIR'AH — FEAR 67

Chapter 5   Te'amei Hamikra — Song or Grammar? 69

Chapter 6   "And he slaughtered" The Fourth Shalshelet:
             Chant and Interpretation 81

Chapter 7   "On the eighth day..."
             The Strangest Trop in Torah 95

Chapter 8   Justice and Mercy...111

GLOSSARY 143

ANNOTATED BIBLIOGRAPHY 151

Blessed is our God, who has created us for His glory, and
set us apart from those who are lost, and has given us a
teaching, a Torah of Truth, planting eternal life in our
midst. May He open our hearts with His Torah, and place
in our hearts love and awe of Him, and to do His will with
a whole heart, so that we will not tire ourselves for nothing,
nor give birth to confusion.

Kedusha Desidra, Daily Prayerbook

Introduction:
The Making of a Torah Reader

THE FIRST FIVE BOOKS OF THE BIBLE
are known by Jews as the Torah, literally The Teaching. At first glance they
may seem a bit of a hodgepodge — stories, epic and mythic material, laws
both ethical and ritual, and passages with seemingly limited relevance
to a modern reader, such as the laws of sacrifices, genealogical material,
and the building plans of an ancient portable shrine. Yet its teachings
have had enduring power and influence. Torah is the foundation of
Rabbinic Judaism: "Turn it and turn it, for everything is in it," the Sages
teach. Torah is also a work of great beauty, featuring complex literary
structures — gripping yarns and soaring poetry. And unlike other works
of antiquity, it can be experienced directly in a living language, without
need of translation.

Saturday morning in any synagogue offers the most primal, most
intensely Jewish experience of sacred text. During the Shabbat service,
we listen to Torah in a tradition going back at least 2500 years to the

1

time of Ezra. Nehemiah 8 describes the first public reading, done with a verse by verse Aramaic translation. The people, recently returned to the Land of Israel from exile in Babylon, were so moved that they wept aloud, before their leaders suggested to them that this should be a time of rejoicing.

Today we connect the public recitation to our annual holiday cycle. Starting at the fall festival of Simchat Torah with the Book of Genesis, we chant weekly portions called *parshiyot* until, by the following Simchat Torah, we have reached the end of Deuteronomy. No sooner do we read Moses' last blessing and the account of his death, than we begin Genesis again the very same day. The public readings are not simply oratorical and dramatic. In a tradition older than the present custom of weekly readings, the Torah is presented to the assembled congregation in an ancient art form — chant. Torah is transformed from written words into Song.

We sing it all. Stories: "And God said to Abraham, 'get you forth'…;" Laws: "When you buy a Hebrew slave, six years shall he work…;" "If an ox gores a man or a woman, who then dies…;" Life maxims: "You shall not take vengeance nor bear a grudge against the children of your people, and you shall love your neighbor as yourself, I am the Lord." We chant the census numbers of Israelite tribes as they begin their wandering through the wilderness. We sing our ancestors' sacrificial rites: "One sheep you shall offer in the morning; the second sheep you shall offer between the evenings…;" We include details such as the number of he-goats contributed by Achiezer, son of Amishadai, Prince of the tribe of Dan, at the dedication of the Tabernacle in the Wilderness. We spend up to five Shabbatot chanting the architectural details involved in building the Tabernacle. When now and then we arrive at genuinely poetic passages, ("Give ear, oh heavens, and I will speak…") the cantillation system often marks these with a more symmetrical, pulsing structure, producing powerful rhythmic effects. It doesn't matter whether or not the text appears intrinsically interesting. In our tradition, everything is read before the congregation in the form of chant. In some places and times, Jewish education was such that almost anyone could step up and read a part of the weekly *parashah* in Hebrew. In Ashkenazi (Western European) synagogues this is no longer the case. One or a few members of the congregation are designated to present the public recitation. One who has learned how to perform the public recitation is called a *ba'al korei* or *ba'al keri'ah*, a master of chanting. This book is the work of one such reader, for whom chanting Torah has been a labor of love and a journey of discovery.

Like most *ba'alei keri'ah*, I am not a clergyman or a professional Judaic scholar. I have spent the last thirty years of my life enjoying the considerable satisfaction of practicing small town family medicine. I have delivered babies, helped people with illnesses and personal crises, and assisted patients and families at the time of death. I am fortunate to have a life partnership with an extraordinary woman who is full of energy and plans. Together we have raised four children in rural East Tennessee. Still, I count among the greatest blessings in my life the opportunity and ability to resonate in song with Torah. For the past 50 years, I have taken great pleasure in chanting the Torah portion aloud in synagogue on Saturday mornings, and have come to feel that this ancient art form is far more than a musical accompaniment to Biblical text. The chanting of a skilled reader can bring to life the power and beauty of Torah text in ways that move the listener. Torah is more than a weekly public presentation of words delivered in musical form. Torah *is* Song, its full meaning bound up with the sound itself. Those who engage consciously with Torah chant as readers or listeners can step into a multi-faceted, intensely enjoyable experience of Scripture. The system of chant notations that guide a reader's emphasis and punctuation also helps a very complex human drama to shine more clearly through the spare, elegant language of Torah.

Since the Torah scrolls in synagogue are written without punctuation or chant markings, the process of preparing a reading involves endless repetition. Anyone who has tried performing a recitation recognizes that a reader must know the portion much better than he/she might have thought at first. There are few public moments worse than standing in front of the congregation, *yad* (pointer) in hand, with the sinking feeling that one is seeing the text for the first time. So in preparation, the reader recites the text over and over. To the thoughtful reader, thoughts come — interpretations, feelings, glimpses of meaning, and perhaps thoughts about the process of chanting Torah in general. My own conviction is that the Torah was from the outset a work of chant and that chant brings the text to life in its most authentic and ancient interpretation. This is hardly a universal opinion, and I have no intent to write an independent work of scholarship to prove my hypothesis. Yet as a careful Torah reader, I reserve the right to comment on academic opinion regarding my craft. After all, the chanting of Torah is an oral folk tradition and has been the province of amateurs for millennia. In most synagogues, lay members of the congregation, not rabbis and cantors, perform this service. And whatever the chant's true origins, and however faithful today's synagogue chant is to its ancient roots, its power to illuminate the Torah is worth exploring.

The Making of a Torah Reader

My personal story as a *ba'al keri'ah* begins at age nine. At Temple Israel in Albany, New York, a remarkable Jewish educator, Phillip "Shraga" Arian, led the junior congregation. Under his guidance, elementary school students would imitate the adult service going on above our heads, including chanting a much-abridged portion of the weekly *parashah*. "Mr. Arian" was my first trop (chant) teacher, and shepherded my earliest steps. My interest in the craft must have been noticed, because within a year, I was allowed to read the somewhat longer portion at Saturday afternoon (*Mincha*) services for the adults. The reading was the beginning of the flood story in Genesis. It was the first of the many times I have been reminded that one must be thoroughly prepared to avoid embarrassment. Public humiliation notwithstanding, I continued to be drawn to chanting.

I was ten years old when my family moved to Israel for three years. In the Ramat Gan neighborhood of Tel Aviv, I attended public religious schools ("*mamlacthi dati,*" which teach both secular and religious subjects), and every Shabbat morning walked to a small neighborhood *shul* (synagogue) with my brother and father. I didn't realize it at the time, but our sojourn in Israel blessed me with three gifts that would prove critical in my growth as a Torah reader. The first was the gift of language. Hebrew does not translate well into English or other languages. Subtleties of meaning, connections of words, wordplay, and the rhythm of speech all get lost in translation. The Torah is a unique work in the Western Canon, written in a language that is still alive today. Although 3000 or so years old, roughly contemporaneous with the works of Homer, the Torah can be picked up and read with basic comprehension by a schoolchild in Israel. It is easier for Israeli third graders to understand Torah than it is for American high school students to decipher *Romeo and Juliet*. Hebrew speakers today have an unparalleled opportunity to access the Torah as a living work and listen to it without an intermediary.

The second gift was the craft of Torah chant, and a flowing trop. The reader we hired in my *shul* in Ramat Gan was a young man studying at Ponevitch Yeshiva who made the forty-minute walk every Shabbat morning from Bnei Brak. He had a plain voice, but was one of the most expert readers I have heard. His pronunciation was crisp and meticulous, his chant perfect in its accuracy. It didn't take long to recognize the quality of the readings. Every reader has slightly differing notes for the different trop. The yeshiva student's version was very simple, and brought out the natural flow and rhythm of the Scriptures.[1] I listened on Shabbat and applied the experience during the week. School began every morning with the daily prayer services. On Monday and Thursday, the service included an abridged Torah reading —a sort of "trailer" for the upcoming Shabbat portion (*parashah*). Volunteers were appreciated, so I read often and began to adopt the *nusach* (melody) used by our reader. Because of constant practice in school, to this day I can read

---

[1] For *ba'alei keri'ah* among the readers: Some of his melodies were not those I hear in the U.S. today. Specific unusual variants include **kadma ve'azla** and **munach legarmeh**. In reading **darga munach revi'a**, he used a different melody than for **darga** in its more usual role preceding **tevir**. Interestingly, Jacobson in his generally authoritative "Complete Guide to Cantillation" (p.373) is not aware of this musical tradition for **darga munach revi'a**, and cites the melody of this trop as an exception to the general rule that a **connector** changes its tune according to the **stop** it precedes.

the first section of any *parashah* on sight. When the time came for my bar mitzvah, the expectation was that I would read the entire *parashah* and its *haftarah* (supplemental portion taken from Prophets) as all my friends from school did. The exercise of preparing a long reading got me past a psychological barrier — I could read an entire *parashah*. It was wonderful timing. In my family we follow the traditional custom of celebrating a child's bar mitzvah on the first Shabbat after the thirteenth Hebrew birthday. As destiny would have it, my bar mitzvah came out on *Shabbat Shira*, the Sabbath of Song, *Parashat Beshalach*. It is the week we recite the Song of Moses and Israel at the Red Sea, at the climax of the Exodus. The portion is full of intense drama told with narrative zest, and the high poetry of the "Song at the Sea." It was a wonderful boost for my skills and love of the craft.

The third gift was the gift of inspiration. One of the strongest and most formative memories from my teen years occurred during the Saturday afternoon service in our small *shul*. On Saturday afternoon, it is customary to read the same preview portion that we read on the upcoming weekday mornings, the beginning of the next Shabbat reading. A young American stranger came in and said he wished to do the Torah reading. The *gabbai* told him that our usual reader had already prepared it. Now our Saturday *Mincha* (afternoon service) reader was not the yeshiva student I mentioned above, but an older member of the *shul*. He read with the old-fashioned European Ashkenazi pronunciation, and was of the school that one should mumble through the reading as fast as possible, with perhaps a token nod to the chant indications. To the *gabbai's* surprise, the American lad persisted in his request, and he was allowed to read. It was *Parashat Noach*, the flood story once again. I remember sitting up and suddenly paying attention as the reading began. The reader had a deep, pleasant voice, and a good musical ear. It was lyrical, rhythmic, fluid, melodic — and gorgeous. That Saturday afternoon moment is what I reach for when I prepare a reading today, and in a sense it is what this book is about.

When my family returned to the United States after I turned thirteen, I continued to be involved in Torah reading in our synagogue, and kept up this involvement throughout college. I could pick up good money reading Torah every other weekend at a nearby *shul*, and the work was more pleasant than washing dishes in the cafeteria. Torah reading became a part time job during my junior and senior year, and for two years after as a graduate student. A *parashah* would take five to seven hours to prepare. I was proud to acquire the discipline of learning an entire portion in a week. I also began to notice that my readings pleased listeners.

From Reader to Writer

My involvement with Torah reading was not enough to keep me from giving in to the spirit of the times and drifting away from Jewish practice. I remember discussing my disenchantment with religion with my Uncle Mendel, Rabbi Emanuel Gettinger of Manhattan, with whom I'd always been close. It was the early seventies, and restraint in advocating for one's new ideology was not in fashion. He asked me to retain the observance of just one *mitzvah* (commandment), so as not to sever the connection with Judaism completely, but I was not interested. What reason was there to maintain any ties to what had become unimportant to me? But I still read Torah on occasion. It was too pleasurable to give up, and I could still impress relatives and friends. I was not aware at the time that chanting the Torah would be the thread of connection that my uncle proposed.

It turned out to be more a lifeline than a thread. I imagined that I was engaged in a mostly esthetic enterprise, a matter of personal enjoyment. But preparation required repetitive recitation of the song of our people, and I was not impervious to the beauty and power of Torah. Now that I am older and presumably wiser, I am struck by how much of my mature moral sense comes from the stories and precepts I have heard since childhood, and how well founded they appear when read once more with the sophistication of adulthood. After a nearly eight-year hiatus, I returned to Jewish practice in a way familiar to many of my generation — after marriage and the birth of a child. I met my future wife, Barbara Levin, in the first year of medical school, and by spring it was obvious to me that we would spend our lives together. That sudden realization and Barb's commitment to the Jewish Tradition began to work changes in my religious sensibility. Our first child, Sunny, was born while Barb and I were residents in family practice in Missouri. Barb and I became involved with our local Jewish community as a couple. The connection to the people of Israel, going back to antiquity and stretching into the distant future, became immediate and palpable. It seemed natural to attend services and read Torah regularly again, first at the University of Missouri, and then in Tennessee, where we moved after finishing our residencies.

In Knoxville I became aware of chant as an art form, and the meaning it brings out in the texts. In the Jewish world, Knoxville is something of a backwater, so its Conservative *shul* has to be self-sufficient. There is a strong sense of belonging, and the community appreciates initiative and participation. The reactions of my friends and fellow congregants, ever ready to listen to Torah reading and to my idiosyncratic reflections, pushed me to refine skills and knowledge. They were willing to put up with far-fetched associations. I once began a *devar Torah* (a short talk commenting on an aspect of Scripture) with the opening of Henry V: "Oh, for a muse of fire…" In discussing how music affects one's mood, I startled the congregation at a daughter's bat mitzvah by opening my talk singing *Kol Nidrei*[2] — in March. The opportunity for unfettered use of imagination, and the imperative to become not only a reader but also a teacher, were demands that led to an increasing investment of energy. This in turn led to an expanded sense of the craft of cantillation, and the power of the chanted verse.

During this period I also happened upon the discipline of the grammar of the *te'amim*. (Hebrew for cantillation marks in Torah chant, also known as trop). By "discipline" I mean academic knowledge — the formal rules

---

[2] This solemn prayer opens the Yom Kippur service in the fall of the year. Its haunting melody would be familiar to all.

that determine how the system of chant notation works to control the flow and stops of verses, allowing it to be used as punctuation. Our rabbi at that time, Mark Greenspan, gave me a copy of an undergraduate college thesis of Rabbi Miles Cohen, "The System of Accentuation of the Hebrew Bible." I already knew this material musically, but Cohen's work was a concise description of the structure I had picked up informally along the way. The intricacy of the grammatical system appealed to my mathematical sensibilities, and amazed me with its elaborate detail. The academic knowledge augmented my understanding and enhanced my enthusiasm for creating an artful presentation.

It has been more than twenty years since this last personal discovery. I have read Torah in many synagogues — "gigs," my daughter Ellie dubbed them. If I'm traveling to another Jewish community over the Sabbath, I am no longer timid or bashful about asking to read Torah in synagogue. There is virtually always a need. The reception is warm, and I can count on appreciation for a good reading with an invitation to return. I am aware that there is always room for improvement and much to learn.

I began to add occasional short introductions before the readings, alerting the congregation to nuances of the readings that they might otherwise miss. Many of these talks involved chant. For example, Leviticus 10 relates that when the Tabernacle in the wilderness is dedicated and becomes operational, Aaron's two eldest sons are incinerated for transgressing the bounds of the sacred. Aaron's brother, Moses, reminds the young men's father of the requirements of holiness. He is to show no sign of mourning. The show must go on. Before attending to the chant, I had always imagined Moses to be the very image of impersonal calm at that moment. The jerky and highly unconventional chant suggests instead that Moses is shaken, and that his composure is forced. (See Chapter 7 for a more detailed discussion).

There was a major side effect to my increased involvement with chanting and teaching Scripture. I developed a nagging need to communicate more widely. I was coming to a different sense of scriptural chant. I felt a responsibility to advocate for an enhanced artful presentation of Torah in its weekly readings. The Torah service should please its audience much like attending a concert or play. This is not merely a matter of idle pleasure. Word-sound, music, and rhythm add to meaning. Rational appreciation is enhanced by art to create an uplifting spiritual experience, a unique blessing of the Jewish tradition. Torah's ancient wisdom has much to say to our own time.

I despaired of having the time for this new mission. I love my communities, both Knoxville and Madisonville, where I reside. Primary care medicine has been enjoyable and fulfilling. I had even found ways of expanding my professional medical interests, teaching students at East Tennessee State University (ETSU) Medical School in Johnson City, and family practice residents in Kingsport. My family life was rich and full, the children energetic and determined, the marriage lively. So where was I to find the time for a writing project?

Enter my wife, Dr. Barbara Levin — with her never-failing sense of the possible and her impatience with whining about obstacles. She encouraged me to take a Sabbatical in order to study and begin writing. After negotiating about reasonable limits to a Sabbatical (namely three months in New York City instead of twelve in Jerusalem), I found myself shuttling between the libraries at the Jewish Theological Seminary and the Riverside Drive apartment of my uncle and aunt, Rabbi Emmanuel and Rachel Gettinger. Out of that precious time came this book.

There were moments of doubt. My wife always brought me back to my original purpose when I became unfocused: "Okay, so say those verses about the killing of the firstborn again." (Ex 12: 29-30). "Now chant them. That difference is what it's about." As my son wrote me in an e-mail: "Remember the message that always gets to people is 'the Torah is song' ... try and keep that message simple." My goal for this book is to share some of my own joy in the process of engaging with "Torah as Song." Within these pages, I hope to offer a straightforward view of how chant works, and explore examples of meaning uncovered by chant. My primary focus is to describe how music enriches the experience of listening to Torah, and allows layers of interpretation to emerge from the text.

It has helped to write in a time when academic texts have begun to excavate the previously neglected area of Torah chant. In his preface to a short instructional book, *The Glory of Torah Reading*, (M.P. Press, 1989; Revised and expanded edition, 1996) Maurice Gellis writes: "With so many books written in English on virtually every other subject in Judaica, the need to fill this void became most compelling." The void is beginning to fill. Most notably Joshua Jacobson's *Chanting the Hebrew Bible: The Complete Guide to the Art of Cantillation* (Jewish Publication Society, 2003) is an invaluable resource in approaching all aspects of chant, including the grammatical, historical, anthropological, and esthetic dimensions. Jacobson describes how the melodies of chant vary widely between (and even within) synagogues around the world. The Ashkenazi European tradition alone recognizes Lithuanian, German, Italian, French, and other styles, while melodic systems developed in the Arabic world of North Africa and the Middle East sound very different. The melodies I use personally are of the Lithuanian tradition common in the Ashkenazi synagogues of Israel and America. Like other readers, I employ methods learned from my teachers in my own style. My melodies and my twentieth-century consciousness color the way I perceive Scriptural passages, though I strive to make those interpretations authentic and consistent with ancient traditions. As Jacobson writes:

> We don't know what the original melodies were for the *te'amim* [chant marks].... throughout the years of the Diaspora these original melodies evolved and mutated as they were passed on orally from one singer to the next. Inevitably the cantillation motifs sung by German Jews began to sound different from those sung by Syrian Jews. Furthermore, even within the community, each *individual* brought something of himself to the *te'amim*. No two Jews chanted the Bible in exactly the same way.

My late father, Mike Gettinger *z'l*, was fond of saying that he did not expect to be known for moving mountains, and expressed the hope that he would be remembered for having budged a grain of sand from here to there. I hope this book will make two grain of sand contributions: First, I would like current and potential Torah readers to recite with greater expression and sensitivity toward the text, increasing their ability to project the beauty of Scripture to their listeners while heightening their own satisfaction with this accomplishment. Second, I hope this satisfaction is reflected in a more pleasurable experience for those listening in synagogues everywhere. I would like the Torah Service, the heart of Saturday morning observance, to consistently move, excite, and inspire Jews all over the world, as I believe it was meant to do.

Acknowledgements

In acknowledging my debts, there is no question of where to start. I would not have begun to write without the support of my wife and partner in family practice, Barbara Levin. I cannot say enough about her, so I will say only this, and it will have to do: she has been my inspiration, my muse, my most serious critic, and the mast to hold fast when faith and confidence wavered. Her personal sacrifice in taking on the additional load to carve out the time for me to study and write can only be imagined by her friends, staff, and colleagues, who recognize how much she always has on her plate.

I am indebted to the staff and patients in my practice in Madisonville, Tennessee, who have taught me so much about life. I also want to thank my congregation in Knoxville, Heska Amuna Synagogue, for their support and encouragement. While many experiences have been formative, it was in Knoxville that I grew into my present powers as a reader. Listener appreciation and willingness to submit to my initial pedagogical efforts was also very helpful. I can truly say that I have learned from many, "but from my students most of all."

My children have informed me that they should be acknowledged for having been patient listeners to my ideas for all their years. In this they are right. But they also deserve a paragraph of their own for their active contributions, for being my best examples of integrating Torah and life, and for being completely uninhibited critics. Years ago, in an earlier draft, I wrote:

> My oldest, Sunny, volunteered for the task suggested by Rabbi Cohen: some of this is very dense and difficult to read. Find someone who truly loves you and would be willing to go over each sentence. Becky has long been a source of inspiration and has given many valuable lessons about spirituality and the meaninglessness of limitations. Ellie has been an unflagging supporter, with a spirit that has seen me through discouraging times, and is the inventor of the concept of Torah reading as "gig." Joe, stuck at home still, has had to put up with more ruminations and discussion than any teenager should. His ability to balance respect with cogent and thoughtful criticism has also been a great help.

It is amazing how one's children grow up. Even Joe has left the nest, and is now chief graphics/blog advisor. In the intervening years all my children have grown in skills and independence. They and their significant others help out in more ways than I can enumerate.

I need to acknowledge my great debt to Rabbi Mark Greenspan, who has been a good friend and critical listener. The Jewish Theological Seminary, and in particular, Chancellor Ismar Schorsch, Rabbi Bill Lebeau and Rabbi Miles Cohen were willing to go out on a limb to let me access the considerable expertise and scholarship of their institution, and to give me of their time. Rabbi Cohen deserves special thanks, for willingness to share his vast knowledge of biblical grammar and chant. His patience as a teacher and willingness to serve as a sounding board for new ideas were invaluable, as were his skepticism and disciplined thought. I will also say a few words of thanks to my uncle, Rabbi Emanuel Gettinger, and his wife, my Aunt Rachel for their wisdom and patience, and for teaching me again the meaning of hospitality in our tradition. Rabbi Gettinger's keen insights into Torah are in a long tradition of great Talmudists' reading of *Mikra*. Dr. Ricky Goldfarb deserves special thanks. My sojourn in New York afforded the opportunity to renew an old friendship, and also led to the unexpected discovery of the last Chumash *shiur* [lesson] in New York City. This daily 6:00 a.m. study session opened every day on the right foot.

Many friends have been willing to give of their time to help refine the writing process. I am indebted to Rabbi Judith Hauptman for early encouragement and criticism. Dr. Gilya Schmidt was overwhelming with her support and critical time. Dr. Clyde Schechter and Rev. Carla Kincannon helped me realize that *The Cloud* could be of interest to those not steeped in the chant tradition. Dr. Heather Hirschfeld was willing to impart of her expertise as an English scholar. Wendy Besmann shared her editorial and writing skills. Dr. Richard Friedman, best known for analyzing and taking apart Scripture, has also given great thought in putting the whole back together. He has also been freely available for the occasional importuning question.

In coming to a final draft, three people deserve a special word of thanks. Wendy Besmann — fan, critic, editor, writing mentor, advisor and plain old friend — has had a lot to do with the final shape of the book and with the fact that it is finished and out in print. Her expert help and support came at critical times. Rabbi Yehoshua Kahan has been my teacher, friend, and *chavruta*.[3] His knowledge has shielded me from some of my more egregious errors. His perspectives have shaped my conceptions. His friendship is treasured. And, finally, thanks to Lynn Fuson, who ushered me into the world of electronic publishing, and helped to turn dream into reality.

It is traditional before beginning Torah study to do so from a sense of obligation and purpose; so we begin Torah study with a series of blessings, which I paraphrase:

---

[3] According to *Wikipedia*, **Chavruta** (from the Aramaic for "friendship" or "companionship") is defined as "a traditional Rabbinic approach to Talumdic study in which a pair of students independently learn, discuss, and debate a shared text. …"

Thank you *Hashem,* our God, King of the universe, who sanctified us with His commandments, and commanded us to engage in words of Torah.

And please make the words of Your Torah pleasant in our mouths and in the mouths of all Your people Israel, and may we and our children and our children's children all know Your Name and be students of Torah for its own sake. Thank you God, who teaches Torah to His people Israel.

In this spirit, I will conclude with thanks to God, for letting me be born into this rich tradition, for a sacred text and the teachings that have followed it, for inspiration, and for preparing my steps.

Preface:
What to Call the Chant and its Notes

The system of symbols[4] that tell
readers how to chant passages of Scripture are sometimes called "accents"
or "trops," particularly by non-Jewish scholars. The Hebrew name for
them is *Te'amei Hamikra* or *te'amim* (singular *ta'am*) for short. The word
I grew up with, and which feels very comfortable to me is "trop," which
I've always pronounced "trup." Like the word "sheep," it is both plural
and singular, and can also mean the entire system of notation and chant
melody. In the book I will use:

- *Te'amei Hamikra* or trop — to mean the entire system of
  notation and their chant tunes;

- *ta'am* or trop (singular) — to mean an individual accent and
  its melody;

- *te'amim* or trop (plural) — to mean several accents or a series of
  them, and their melodies.

There are two type of *te'amim*. Eighteen of the twenty-seven accent signs
are "disjunctives," which serve as a very intricate system of punctuation,
more precise and subtle than periods and commas. The rest are

---

[4] In this entire book, we will deal only with the "twenty-one books," that is, the
Hebrew Bible excluding the three "Emet" books: Job, Proverbs, and Psalms. These three
books have a different chant system, and are not recited in public. As a consequence,
no one knows their melodies, or how they were performed. In counting the number
of remaining books in the *Tanakh* as twenty-one, one counts Samuel, Kings, and
Chronicles as one and not two books each; and the twelve "minor prophets" are
counted as one book.

"conjunctives" and lead in to the disjunctives. It gets complicated, because the disjunctives have four ranks of greater and lesser pauses. In Hebrew this terminology does not sound as technical as it does in English. The disjunctives are called "Kings" or "Stops," and the conjunctives are called "Servants" or "Connectors." For clarity, I will use the terms **stops** and **connectors,** and describe ranks of stops only when necessary.

Hebrew or Yiddish terms used in the book are briefly defined when they first appear in the text, but more detailed explanations and commentary on those terms can be found in the *Glossary*.

Translating the Name of God

These days any book dealing with Scripture in translation seems to require an explanation of the author's choice for rendering the most common Hebrew name for God in the Torah, the four Hebrew letters YHWH, which are known in English as the Tetragrammaton. Jews do not pronounce this name today in reading Scripture aloud. The traditional view is that its pronunciation aloud was reserved to the High Priest on Yom Kippur, the holiest day of the calendar, and only after extensive purification. Instead in a public reading we substitute the word *Adonai* [literally, "my Lord"], and Orthodox Jews do not utter even this word except with sacred purpose, such as prayer or public reading of Torah. In private conversation or even during Torah study they substitute yet again another word, *Hashem* [literally, "the Name"]. There are several other names for God in the Torah, but one (*Elohim*) is far more common than the others. Of the many options for translators, the most common are:

	YHWH	*Elohim*
King James, Revised Standard, JPS, Alter	The Lord	God
Fox, Friedman	YHWH	God
Art Scroll	HASHEM	God

I have followed a fourth path, the path of inconsistency. "God" is my comfortable word for speaking of the Deity in English, and I have generally translated both Hebrew names in this fashion. For me it is a matter of remaining as intimate as I can be with an English text of Torah. I have occasionally used "the Lord" when I needed an extra syllable for rhythmic purposes. Feel and comfort were my overriding priorities, though I recognize the valid reasons a particular translator may have for his choice. All recognize that each of these translations is a compromise.

PART ONE
AHAVAH — LOVE

The teaching of God is perfect, reviving the spirit.
The decrees of God are sure, making the simple wise.
The precepts of God are just, gladdening the heart.
The command of God is clear, enlightening the eyes.
The fear of God is pure, enduring forever.
The laws of God are true, altogether just.
They are more precious than gold, even the purest gold;
and sweeter than honey and the drippings of
the honeycomb.

Psalm 19

Chapter 1
Biblical Chant —
Rhythmic Speech

THE PSALMIST SAYS OF THE TEACH-
ings of the Torah: "they are sweeter than honey and the drippings of the
honeycomb." That "sweetness" flows not only from the brilliance of the
ideas, but also from the sensual pleasure of listening to words crafted
beautifully and set to music. The Torah makes its public appearance
in an age of emerging literacy, in which there were no means of mass
producing texts. The beauty of the sound of Torah is intentional. It is
designed to hold the attention of a people who primarily hear rather than
read the content.

The notion of pleasure in the pure sound of Scripture's language is
implicit in the work of sensitive English translators, from Tyndall, the
herald of the King James Bible, to the present day. In the past century,

translators of the Bible began to write of the challenge of capturing not only the literal meaning of Scriptures but also their feel, so as to uncover the pleasure in listening to the Bible. Robert Alter wrote in the preface to his translation of Genesis: "Biblical Hebrew … has a distinctive music, a lovely precision of lexical choice, a meaningful concreteness, and a suppleness of expressive syntax, that by and large have been given short shrift by translators with other goals."[5] He also writes, "An important reason for the magnetic appeal of these stories when you read them in the Hebrew is the rhythmic power of the words that convey the story."[6]

The power of the rhythmic speech of Torah was examined with passionate admiration by two leading Jewish thinkers of the 20th century: Martin Buber and Franz Rosenzweig. Both are known for contributions to Jewish and Zionist thought, and Buber has had influence in the wider world of theology and philosophy. What is less well known is their consuming preoccupation with translating the Bible. In 1925, they began work on a German translation of the *Tanakh*, the Hebrew Bible. They were self conscious about their project and left a precious legacy — a series of essays titled *Scripture and Translation*[7] commenting on the art of translating Scripture. The noted English translator of the Bible Everett Fox was inspired by their work. In the introduction to the English version of the essays, he writes that *Scripture and Translation* "is not merely about biblical poetics, close reading, translation theory, or cultural history — although it deals with all these issues in depth and in an entirely original manner.… It is above all a passionate, even utopian plea for the revival of the Bible's ability to speak in living words, to renew what Buber called 'the dialogue between heaven and earth.'"

The Hebrew Scriptures are noted for their eloquence and power of expression. When George Orwell in his essay "Politics and the English

---

[5] Alter, essay: "The Bible in English and the Heresy of Explanation," in *The Five Books of Moses: A Translation with Commentary*, p. xiv.

[6] Alter, essay: "The Bible in English and the Heresy of Explanation," in *The Five Books of Moses: A Translation with Commentary*, p. xlii.

[7] Everett Fox, "The Book in its Contexts" in Buber and Rosenzweig, *Scripture and Translation*, p. xiii.

Language" reaches for an example of vivid metaphoric writing to contrast with banal contemporary prose, he picks a passage from Ecclesiastes. "I returned and saw under the sun that the race is not to the swift, nor the battle to the strong, neither yet bread to the wise, nor yet riches to men of understanding, nor yet favour to men of skill; but time and chance happen to them all." Orwell wrote a parody of these same lines in twentieth century English and concluded by lamenting the inability of modern writers to attain this level of literary skill.

The quality of the Torah's word craft is often missed. The science fiction writer Isaac Asimov, in the introduction to his commentary on Shakespeare, makes the not-uncommon association between Shakespeare and the Bible as the two preeminent works in the Western Canon. He goes on to say that Shakespeare is in one respect superior. Not only does it offer dazzling insights into the human condition, but it also sounds beautiful, even when heard without regard to meaning. It is not hard to imagine how he came to this opinion, since he was more likely to encounter a fine presentation of Shakespeare than an artful chanting of Torah. Yet as much as I appreciate Shakespeare's language, it is no match for a well-chanted Torah portion with respect to glory of sound. Alliteration, assonance, rhythm, and melody are brought to bear in the service of a text notable for its clarity, elegance, bluntness, and vivid description. Shakespeare, writing for the stage, designed his words to be complemented by the magic of actors and visual effects. Torah, developed in a time when effective oral transmission was absolutely critical, depends entirely on sound to transmit its message.

Artful recitation is important not just as a matter of pleasure, but also for clarity of expression and power. A sage once admonished that one should learn: "*mipisofrim, ve'lo mipise'farim,*" literally, learn "from the mouths of scholars and not the mouth of [their] books." The common sense of this admonition is clear. It is the difference between reading about a subject and taking a class in which the material is presented orally. Oral presentation permits emphasis, clarification, and dramatization. I read Torah with a conscious awareness of the need to reach listeners. Verses must be parsed correctly and clearly. Dialogue should have the necessary dramatic feel; words said in anger should sound angry, for example. The rhythm of poetic passages can be brought out. The lists, enumerations, and genealogies in the Torah also have literary content and are composed with sound quality in mind. A good reading — musical, rhythmic, and flowing — brings these otherwise dry passages to life.

Rosenzweig emphasized the importance of receiving the Bible as a spoken rather than written work. The essay "Scripture and Word" begins, "Every word is a spoken word." Rosenzweig along with Buber[8] expressed the firm opinion that the Hebrew Bible was originally spoken (I would suggest, *chanted*), and that this was the way in which the people related to it — as a performed work. He asks us to think of the written text as we think of the script of a play. Is the play in the script, or in the performance? When the primary focus becomes the text, "It becomes the word's ruler and hindrance. It becomes Holy Scripture." He speaks of the need for the book to be alive, and avoid becoming "literature:"

> The Bible alone among all books of the literary epoch … demands a pre-literary mode of reading — that is what the Hebrew word for reading means… the "*keri'ah*" or "calling out." It is in response to this command that in all worship, scripture is customarily read aloud; it is in the service of this command that Luther has recourse to the spoken language of the people [i.e., translation].…. We must free from beneath the logical punctuation, that is sometimes its ally and sometimes its foe, the fundamental principle of natural, oral punctuation: the act of breathing.[9]

In the same spirit, Martin Buber, commenting on the Exodus story notes:

> That this early saga, close as it is to the time of the event, tends to assume rhythmical form can well be understood. It is not due solely to the fact that enthusiasm naturally expresses itself in rhythm. Of greater importance is the basic idea characterizing this

---

[8] Buber and Rosenzweig, *Scripture and Translation*, p. 42.

[9] Buber and Rosenzweig, *Scripture and Translation*, p. 42. It is no accident that the traditional Hebrew term closest to the word "Scripture" is *Mikra*, or "that which is called out." By contrast "Scripture" derives from the Latin root "to write."

stage of human existence that historical wonder can be grasped by no other form of speech save that which is rhythmically articulated, of course in oral expression (a basic concept which is closely associated with the time-old relation between religion and magic.) This is sustained by the wish to retain unchanged for all time the meaning of the awe-inspiring things that had come about; to which end a transmission in rhythmic form is the most favorable condition.

An urge to transmit this sense of "historical wonder," to enable "the revival of the Bible's ability to speak in living words, to renew …the dialogue between heaven and earth" were imperatives that spurred the two German translators. Their work would be the last Jewish book printed in Germany in the early twentieth century. Then destruction befell the German Jewish community. But the spirit of their work lives on. They had immeasurable influence on the current generation of English translators. More importantly, Buber also labored tirelessly on the Zionist enterprise, and today the *keri'ah*, the calling out of the Hebrew Scriptures is again performed in a living tongue. The urgency of its message is no less than it has ever been. Buber and Rosenzweig noticed that the rhythmic cadences of the spoken word enhance the power of the text, but they miss one component of the art of presentation of Torah in chant. For full effect we need to hear not only its rhythm, but also its music.

Surely, this instruction, which I enjoin upon you this day, is not too baffling for you, nor is it far off. It is not in the heavens, that you should say, "Who can go up to the heavens and get it for us and impart it to us, that we may observe it? Neither is it beyond the sea, that you should say, "Who can cross to the other side of the sea and get it for us and impart it to us, that we may observe it? No, the thing is very close to you, in your mouth and in your heart to do it.

Deut 30, 11-14, adapted from JPS

Chapter 2
"This song will be a witness..." (Deut 31)
The Melodies of Biblical Chant

BUBER AND ROSENZWEIG CONCEN-trated on the way Chant is a rhythmic form of speech. They found the traditional musical accents, the *Te'amei Hamikra*, better guides to interpretation than the conventional punctuation of the text. Writing in twelfth century Spain, the poet and philosopher Yehuda Halevi expressed a similar view:

...They signify the places where the speaker intended to pause between two thoughts or the place where he intended to connect words together. They separate question from answer, subject from predicate, words spoken in haste from more deliberate speech, command from supplication. One could write volumes on this subject.[10]

---

[10] Yehuda Halevi, quoted in Jacobson, *Chanting the Hebrew Bible*, p. 10.

Everett Fox, when reading Torah in synagogue, recites with the cadenced rhythms of the *te'amim*, but without their tunes. It is an effective technique that brings out some of the beauty of the text much as a spirited poetry reading can enhance the experience of verse.

Still, as resonant as a dramatic, rhythmic reading can be, melody has an independent effect on listeners. The result is further augmentation of the power and the beauty of a work of acknowledged high literary expression. Music leads to heightened drama. Stories come to life. Joseph's anguish can be felt. The exchanges between Moses and Pharaoh present increased tension. The stand at the Red Sea comes off with a grander sweep. Music also moves us in ways that plain speech does not. It is an emotion amplifier, making happy moments more joyful, sad ones more mournful. In describing Torah as song, I am consciously connecting it with the age-old enterprise of linking words and music. From ditties, advertising jingles, and popular compositions to the high culture of opera and Bach's B Minor Mass, humans take pleasure in combining melody and text. The pleasure of listening to song has multiple parts. Listeners take pleasure in the sound of the words, in the music, and in the interaction between the two. There is also the intellectual (rational and emotional) satisfaction of ideas cleverly arrayed and insights elegantly conveyed, and these too can be acted upon and augmented by the music.

To quote a remark of Amichai Lau-Lavie, whose organization *Storahtelling* uses improvisational theater to bring Torah to life: "Music lets you wrap your right brain around all that left brain stuff." The Torah not only contains profound truths about human nature and our relationship to the divine; it is also crafted to reach the human spirit on many levels, not just the rational. It is critical to the Torah's mission that it be heard on the level of emotion and motivation. To accomplish this, it couches sophisticated teaching about life and human nature in gripping, complex and morally ambiguous stories. It reaches poetic heights that Hebrew writers emulate to this day. And it combines text — stories, poems, and teachings — with the uncanny beauty expressed in the music of an ancient chant tradition. Music, even without words, has effects on the human psyche and spirit that are still little understood (why we perceive some melodies as sad and others as happy, for instance). Combine music with words, and both are changed.

By way of illustration, take for example a slow song such as the Beatles' "Yesterday." Note that the pace is uneven. ("Yesterday/All my troubles seemed so far away/Now it looks as though they're here to stay.") Some words are drawn out; other phrases are run through trippingly. The title word hangs in the air for a long instant, and returns with different rhythms, emphasizing the yearning for what was lost. "Yesterday" uses both rhythmic speech and melody to express intensified emotion — longing, sadness. In a similar fashion, Torah chant utilizes musical and rhythmic effects to impart emphasis and heightened emotion. Musical effects can be very expressive in stories, and can lead to enjoyment of texts that would not usually be considered literary.

There is a standing joke in our synagogue, following Shabbat morning services: I tell my friends which passage I liked so much in that particular Sabbath reading and why it is one of my favorites. The invariable rejoinder is, "They're all your favorites." The truth is that I enjoy a good list as much as the best yarn, or as much as the loftiest philosophical truth expressed in vivid metaphor. I have always enjoyed reading lists. Some of this is intangible — a matter of the Torah's wonderful way with rhythm and sound. But as I gained in experience, I came to recognize that the lists also have "literary" value, and significance that is not necessarily foreign to modern sensibilities. Chanted in Hebrew, they can be imbued with the emotional overtones that help us to understand their importance in Torah. Reduce them to words on paper, translate them, and they become flat and boring. At the end of one synagogue service some years ago, a listener commented that she found the Torah reading "moving." I was surprised: we had just read the list of the names of the sons of Esau. My friend Wendy Besmann commented on reading the census in Numbers:

> I had a sudden visceral sense of the possibilities of "Torah lists" during the reading of the census in the Book of Numbers. I had a flash of how it must have looked and sounded: Hundreds of

thousands of men are gathered around the Tabernacle in tribal formation, carrying spears and waving their standards. Ringed around them is the rest of Israel, well over a million in all. The chief of the census bellows out, "And the tribe of Issachar is numbered 46,500!" The tribe roars out its pride, beating spears on the earth, shaking timbrels, raising its banner as the troops march into their appointed position for the long journey. The shouts of celebration rise up twelve times as the tribes become one unified host to guard the Tabernacle of God's Presence among the people. It must have been amazing. Centuries later we tend to page through this stuff, waiting to get to the more interesting stories. The chant can show us how it might have been.

Music and emotion, an example from Genesis

The stories of Genesis are among the most famous in Western literature. Drama, pathos, characterization are thousands of years ahead of their time. They are shining examples of the storyteller's art. Presented in chant, they are even more beautiful and stirring. Jacobson cites the view of an Italian Renaissance rabbi, Samuel Archivolti, on how music can affect the experience of listening to text. Writing in an era destined to blow open possibilities for musical expression, Archivolti described the power of music to alter presentation of words:

> ...by melodic changes we are able to distinguish between pause and continuation, a fast tempo and a slow one, between joy and sadness, astonishment and fear, and so forth. And this is the most excellent type of melody in music, for not only does it consider the ear's pleasure, but also strives to give spirit and soul to the words that are sung.[11]

Highlighting and coloring points of emotional intensity is a standard use of music to this day. When the operatic diva breaks from recitative to aria, when the actor in a musical begins to sing, they are generally not advancing the plot, but rather giving us a more intimate and detailed

---

[11] Jacobson, *Chanting the Hebrew Bible*, p. 515.

glimpse of their internal state — their joys, pains, and struggles. Similarly, when chant departs from rhythmic simplicity, it is worth listening for musical effects. A familiar example illustrates how music enhances the Torah's stories. As I have spoken to people about this project, many *ba'alei keri'ah* have shared with me moments during their readings that have given them immediate pleasure. One such "trop moment" was cited by several readers for its emotional intensity, brought out by the music of the chant.

Genesis 27 tells of Isaac's blessing his two sons, Jacob and Esau. Isaac is old. Sensing that the end may be not far off, he asks Esau to hunt game and prepare him a meal, and then receive the blessing of the firstborn. Esau is a powerful man, his father's pride and joy. The twins' mother, Rebecca, has other plans. Her favorite is the gentler Jacob. She senses correctly that the younger son should receive the primary blessing. Perhaps she also recalls the oracle that foretold their birth: "Two nations are in your womb…and the greater will serve the younger." Taking advantage of her husband's failing eyesight; she dresses Jacob in Esau's finery, and puts goatskins on his arms and the back of his neck, lest his smooth skin betray him to his father's touch. The ruse is successful: "The voice is the voice of Jacob, but the hands are the hands of Esau," Isaac says, and blesses the younger son. The story comes to a climax when Esau, successful in the hunt, enters his father's tent with the meal he has prepared.

"Who are you?" Isaac asks.

"I am your firstborn son, Esau," is the reply.

"And Isaac trembled — a great trembling." Having previously recognized Jacob's voice, he must have known the answer to his next question: "Who then is the game hunter, and he brought me, and I ate of it all before you came, and I blessed him? He will in fact be blessed."

Esau recognizes that he has once again been tricked by his brother, and then breaks down in tears: "Do you have only one blessing, father? Bless me too, father."

There is a resentful momentary peace as Isaac gives Esau a lesser blessing than he had intended for his firstborn son. Any judgment we might have made regarding Esau's subsequent murderous intent is tempered by the intense love and respect he accords his father, and his grief at losing his intended blessing.

How trop works will be the subject of Chapter 4. For our present purpose, it is enough to know that the chant accents on verse 33 — "And Isaac trembled a great trembling; and he said, who then…" — are unusual, and caught the attention of my reader friends. The trop on these words is designed to wake its audience, calling attention and dramatizing Isaac's emotional state. As one reader said, "I could feel the tremor in Isaac's voice."

Genesis 27 is one of many instances of chant indicating emotional coloration of a story. This story is occasionally read as a fable of good versus evil — the righteous Jacob claiming his birthright from the wicked Esau. The Art Scroll Chumash, for example, emphasizes this strain of rabbinic interpretation. But the Sages also saw in this story a less than blameless Jacob, and even recognized the merits of Esau in his veneration of his father.[12] Genesis stories are not generally fables or mythic legends but psychologically complex, morally ambiguous works that surpass most modern fiction for literary quality and startling insights into human nature. Here is Richard Friedman's comment on verse 33:

> The sensitivity that is shown here for the feelings of Isaac and of Esau indicates how wrong it is to excuse Jacob and sully Esau in our interpretations. The text reveals that Rebekah's plan and Jacob's actions have caused a deep hurt. Rather than excuse them, the story will show how these things are resolved later through maturing and forgiveness

---

[12] *Devarim Rabbah,* Chapter 2.

Friedman did not need chant to recognize that the Torah has portrayed a complex and difficult story, but dramatization of the story in chant renders audible the story's tension and regard for the feelings of its characters. Trop expresses in music the same sensitivity that Friedman finds in the text. The effect was obvious to my friends the Torah readers, and, it is to be hoped, to their listeners. When storytellers tells a story, when actors acts out a play, when good readers reads a poetic or literary work, their expression brings out qualities such as feeling, dramatic tension, emphasis. When a singer sings with expression, an audience can be moved to tears or to elation. Torah chant often gives cues that signal a dramatic moment. The Torah reader should imagine him/herself as a master storyteller or singer, bringing the dimension of song to a text whose wonder is continually unfolding.

So now write this song and teach it to the children of Israel, place it in their mouths; so that this song will become a witness for Me among the children of Israel…. And Moses wrote this song on that day, and he taught it to the children of Israel.

Deuteronomy 31: 19 and 22

Chapter 3
The Origins of Torah Chant

"SO NOW WRITE THIS SONG AND teach it to the children of Israel, place it in their mouths." Israel, after forty years of wandering, is about to enter the Promised Land. Moses has already passed the mantle of leadership to Joshua, son of Nun. He is told to transmit a last caution in the form that is most suitable for a compelling message that must endure — Song. The "Song of Moses," Chapter 32 of Deuteronomy, is one of the treasures of the art of biblical chant.

I have chosen to translate the word *shira* as "song" rather than "poem," because my intuition is that music was an inherent part of the composition, and not a later addition to text. That is to say, I have come to feel through years of chanting that Scriptures *are* Chant, are born in Chant, and are best heard as inseparable from Chant. The Torah is not a libretto to which a later generation added a musical score. The composers or Composer wrote and thought in Chant.

In advocating for this point of view I am going to avoid taking sides in the current argument over the origin of Scripture. Orthodox Jewish opinion holds that Torah was handed down to Moses at Sinai. Orthodox believers also accept the notion that *Te'amei Hamikra*, the chant indications, were given at Sinai. The *te'amim* thus serve to preserve a faithful oral presentation of Torah from generation to generation. On the other hand, the liberal Jewish denominations accept to varying degrees the assumptions of academic biblical scholarship. This viewpoint conceives of Torah as originating in an oral tradition, with several strands eventually written down and finally pulled into present day form by a redactor (editor). Even according to this perspective, it is at least plausible that the Torah in its original oral form was a chanted work.

Chant was pervasive in the ancient world. In what has been termed the Axial Age (800-200 BCE), around the world from Greece to India to Japan, communities chanted sacred works. The *Jewish Encyclopedia* (in the article "Masoretic Accents") identifies common elements of "cantillation" from a variety of traditions, such as Vedic recitation in India or Buddhist recitation in Japan:

> This cantillation is based on strict conventions handed down by oral tradition (which were described explicitly only in the respective Middle Ages of each culture)[13]...a basic similarity...can still be recognized in all such practices throughout the Asian continent, including all Jewish traditions throughout the Diaspora.... This "pan-Asiatic" style must already have been present in cantillated Bible reading in the synagogue preceding the period in which the written accents began to be developed.

Ancient editions of Homer's epics also come with accent signs, the exact usage of which died with the decline of Greek civilization. Roman orators, who admired Classical works, decried the Greek custom of performing them in chant rather than declaiming in the manner of

---

[13] In other words, chant exists as an oral tradition for centuries, perhaps millennia, before its formal rules are written down. The origins of chant are veiled by the mists of time.

speech. It is reasonable to infer that the ancient Hebrews also chanted their sacred texts.

In addition to historical considerations, I have a more compelling personal reason for my conviction that Torah was composed as a chanted work. Repetition and practice has fed the deep intuition of one who has read passages aloud thousands of times. In making it a priority to provide an expressive, satisfying reading for the congregation, I learned to rely on trop for indications of rhythmic expression, phrasing, and dramatic emphasis. The process of preparing a chanted reading culminates in a clear sense of the passage, what it seems to be saying, how it works. Trop has been for me, as my friend Wendy Besmann put it, "a magnificent doorway to understanding the inner meaning of Torah text." Now it is not essential that the reader accept the notion that trop is contemporaneous with Torah and inextricable from the text. The reader can still appreciate the singing of the Torah as a thing of beauty, and the interpretations I have derived from the readings as interesting. But if trop also taps into what I have dared call the "original literary intent of the Torah," then analysis of trop becomes more than a foray into the interpretations of sages and medieval scribes.

There is a common misconception that Torah chant was originated by an obscure group of scholar/scribes known as the Masoretes at the end of the first millennium of the Common Era. This is incorrect. The history of chant and chant signs is clearly much older. As the Jewish Encyclopedia points out, "the system of accent signs and vowel signs and their functions was based on existing practices, not only of the punctuation and grammatical basis…but also of its musical rendition." We know from the Talmud that the tradition of chanting Torah was already well established in Mishnaic times a thousand years before written notation for trop. Hand signals were originally used to convey the chant melodies. The Talmud[14] contains a discussion of the reason one is supposed to use the left hand in wiping [one's bottom] and not the right. Rabbi Nachman ben Isaac and Rabbi Akiva voice the opinion that this

---

[14] Berachot 62

is "because one points with it [i.e., the right hand] to the accents [trop] in the scrolls." The presence of hand signals suggests that in Rabbi Akiva's time (second century C.E.) the chant system was complicated enough to merit memory aids.

For centuries, Torah chant was an entirely oral tradition. All this changed in the last century of the first millennium. Over centuries, a group of scribes living in Tiberias on the Sea of Galilee became known for their reliability and fidelity in keeping the tradition of how the sacred scrolls of the Torah were to be written and how they were to be read. There were a handful of families, who passed down knowledge of recording the Scriptures on parchment by hand from generation to generation. They were known as the Masoretes. We are indebted to them not only for the preservation of the written text in its present form, down to where to insert paragraph breaks, but also for leaving us two great inventions.

The first is called the Masoretic system of vocalization. Long before the Masoretes, the ancient Hebrews had made universal literacy possible with an alphabetical innovation.[15] Other alphabets of the time consisted only of consonants. In the Hebrew alphabet, three consonant letters, *yod*, *heh*, and *vav*, were to be used also as vowels, like the letter "y" in English. But these partial vowels did not resolve the dilemma of precisely how to determine a word's pronunciation. For example, the letter *vav*, used as a vowel, could be pronounced either "ooh" or "oh." Another example: in Genesis 43, Joseph's half brothers return to Egypt with his full brother Benjamin. We are told that his merciful feelings were quickened toward *a.ch.y.v.* This can be read either *echav* [his brothers] or *achiv* [his brother; i.e., Benjamin]. The Masoretic tradition specifies the latter reading, a detail with significant import in the story. The Masoretes needed a system to guarantee that Torah would be read correctly each time. They added a system of dots and lines ("diacritical marks" in linguistic parlance) above and below the letters to indicate precisely how a word should be

---

[15] This process is described by the linguist Joel Hoffman in a popular work, *In the Beginning: A Short History of the Hebrew Language.*

pronounced. In this way the accurate, reproducible pronunciation of the Hebrew text was assured.

The Masoretes' second great invention was the written notation for Torah chant, *Te'amei Hamikra.*

About the year 930 C.E., in the town of Tiberias in northern Israel, the Masorete Aharon Ben-Asher took a manuscript of the entire *Tanakh,* and wrote on it the vowels and the symbols for the *te'amim.* The manuscript was in the form of a codex. That is, it was written by hand on parchment, but in book rather than scroll form. It came to be known as the Aleppo Codex, after the city in Syria where it ended up during the Middle Ages. Before reaching Syria, this masterwork landed for a time in Alexandria, Egypt. Moses Maimonides, the preeminent Jewish scholar of his generation, came across the codex about the year 1200 in Egypt, and recognized its quality. With his stamp of authority this text quickly became the official version of the entire Jewish world. It was not the first or the only text from that period to showcase the Masoretes' fully developed system for vocalization and chant, but it was a document of historic significance. It is the only "later" document to be displayed in the Israel Museum's Scroll of the Book pavilion, which exhibits the Dead Sea Scrolls.

The Masoretic trop notation must have represented the musical tradition of its time effectively, since it caught on quickly. Some have questioned how faithfully the Masoretes transmitted the ancient traditions. Robert Alter says concerning the notation for the vowel system invented by the Masoretes: "There was, however, a continuous tradition for recitation of the texts on which the Masoretes drew, and anyone who has listened to the Masoretic Text read out loud can attest to its strong rhythmic integrity, which argues that its system of pronunciation was by no means an arbitrary imposition."[16] The same can be said for their system of musical accents, *Te'amei Hamikra.* This view, that the Masoretes did not invent the system of musical chant, but simply devised a clear and authoritative notation for it, fits what we know about them. They

---

[16] Alter, *The Five Books of Moses,* Introduction, p. xliii.

practiced their scribal craft anonymously for generations, with virtually no prominent individuals among them whose names we recall today. We have no record of large academies attracting students, but rather a collection of families whose traditions were passed down from father to son. Even their name is suggestive of their role. "Masorete" derives from the Hebrew root *m.s.r,* to transmit. Their work was widely accepted throughout the Jewish world. They were regarded as faithful transmitters of the tradition, and, as such, could not have had an interpretive agenda of their own.

Their agenda, apparent from their work, consisted of three objects: fidelity of text, fidelity of pronunciation (vocalization), and fidelity of chant (grammar and music). Not only did they make sure that a Torah scroll from 15th century Persia has the same words broken into the same paragraphs as one in today's New York, but they also substantially insured that a *ba'al keri'ah* today will utter the same words and parse the sentences the same way in public chant. Scholars (for example, see Hoffman) question whether the Masoretic vocalization accurately reflects the pronunciation of Hebrew in Biblical times. This is not exactly the right question. The Masoretes would not have been concerned with the language of the street, but rather with the language of presentation of a public performance. Even today, we know from our art forms that pronunciation of Shakespearean English or the French of the *Comedie Française* follow different rules than those of daily speech. It is this "high" Hebrew that was the Masoretes' preoccupation. In the face of differences of culture and time, and without printing presses to replicate text and notation, their work was highly successful.

As indicated above, the existence of hand signals to indicate *te'amim* means there must have been a cadre of readers who painstakingly learned the chant melodies, and who would be responsible for indicating them to those less skilled in this art in the community. In early years, transmission of the chant was accomplished without a written notation indicating how the text was to be sung. It is hard to imagine Torah chant's survival to the present day without its Masoretic notation. In committing an oral musical tradition to writing, the Masoretes established this tradition securely for the ages. Communities scattered about the earth now had a common written version of the text, complete with vowels and trop. The immediate acceptance of Masoretic notation throughout the Jewish world is one more testimony that it accurately reflected accepted practice. Two centuries later, the noted medieval commentator Rashi, writing in northeastern France, would comment on the passage in the Talmud referring to using the left hand for wiping. He tells his European audience that the passage is referring to an old practice of using the right hand to indicate *Te'amei Hamikra*, and adds that he actually saw this practice once when a Jew from Palestine came through his community. Despite the absence of printing and rapid communication, cheironomy — using hand signals to aid the Torah reader — was a dim memory in most of the Jewish world just two centuries after Aharon Ben-Asher penned his fateful work.

Torah Chant: the evolution of melodies

If the origins of chant notation are clear, the source of the melodies is more elusive. I am occasionally surprised by the question of whether the melodies are the same as they were thousands of years ago. The answer is: clearly not. There are no traces or musical records from antiquity, and although from time to time someone claims to have rediscovered the ancient melodies, it is clearly a matter of conjecture. As a *ba'al keri'ah*, I am aware of how I myself have changed what I received, taking tunes and methods from different readers, and adapting them to my own style. While there is no authoritative music, nevertheless there are rules and a sense of what is appropriate. From age to age the responsibility for recitation has rested on lay members of the community; the congregation is the only judge of correctness. As a consequence, the music varies from community to community, and even between readers in the same synagogue.

What must happen in an oral tradition is that melodies alter incrementally as Jews pass from age to age and society to society. The "musical ear" of a given time was no doubt of some influence, and this is probably one of the secrets of the chant's survival by adaptation of the chant.

The Israeli musicologist Hanoch Avenary remarks on the resemblance of Ashkenazi chant tunes today to melodies from medieval European folk tunes of the year 1200, and suggests that these secular, gentile melodies were imposed on Ben-Asher's system of *te'amim* to make them singable by the "ordinary" synagogue attendee.[17] I would suggest a more modest proposition: the secular music of one's community influences the musical ear of the reader, and likely exerts subtle effects on the tunes in synagogue, and possibly vice versa. In any case, it is clear that until recently, the music of *Te'amei Hamikra* was not set down in a form that would let it become frozen in time. What must happen is that as the music of the world around us changes, the melodies of the chant change in ways that suit the taste of each particular culture and time. I like to think of my tunes as western and modern enough to be musically sensible to my listeners, with enough dash of eastern flavor to transport the listener to the Middle Eastern desert of 3,000 years ago.

In contrast to modern listeners, the listeners of ancient times were used to hearing their stories and their poems sung or chanted. There were no books, and few scrolls. The preservation and transmission of a communal story depended on public recitation of sagas and family stories. People would have been attuned to this medium. It was all around them, part of the fabric of their lives. Chant patterns, departures from those patterns, special highlights, would catch their attention in a recitation. And they would take pleasure in the listening, much as we do today when we hear stories and songs. The surprise is that biblical chant has proved a durable way to transmit ancient wisdom. Although other chant forms have passed out of western civilization, Torah chant remains a vibrant, living tradition.

But is it authentic?

When I stand in front or in the midst of a congregation, *yad* [pointer] in hand, about to proclaim Torah to a group of my people, I imagine myself as part of a continuous tradition of recitation, receding into the distant

---

[17] Hanoch Avenary, *The Ashkenazy Tradition of Biblical Chant between 1500 and 1900.*

past and stretching out into the future. This is sacred work, because the word is important and still has much to say to the world. It must be recited clearly, with correct inflection, pronunciation, and punctuation. It should be musical and dramatic; it should move its listeners. If the melodies I am singing are not those of two thousand years ago, how can I be sure that I am an authentic modern voice of an ancient tradition?

This question is particularly pointed in a time when Scripture means different things to different people. Some think of it as outmoded and irrelevant. For others it is a profound ancient voice worth mining for its pearls of wisdom, while discarding the parts that are jarring to modern sensibilities. Yet others hear it as the literal word of God, with each reading a new revelation. Some have found their best entry through the realm of secular scholarship, which separates different strands of authorship of the text, and uses archeology and history to shed light on the differing perspectives and agendas of the various authors. What does it even mean, then, to ask: "Is the chant authentic?"

And yet for me, this is a central preoccupation. The *ba'al keri'ah* cannot get bogged down in questions of origins of text. The mission is to bring the text to life: all of it — stories, lists, and laws — whether he or she sees their beauty and relevance or not. Let others make their personal decision about how to relate to the text, but only after hearing its best, most piercing, musical presentation. When I ask about authenticity, I am asking whether or not I have inadvertently changed the meaning. Scribes faithfully preserve the written text. A Torah scroll in Manhattan in the year 2000 is virtually identical to one from Yemen at the end of the first millennium. Chant serves oral presentation like the scribal tradition serves fidelity in written transmission. *Te'amei Hamikra* make sure that faithfully, generation after generation, we punctuate the text in the same way. We avoid shifting a comma, or even a lesser pause. But music can also alter meaning, and chant traditions have diverged. When I sing a passage today, is the musical effect on the listener recreating faithfully the experience of a listener of thousands of years ago, or have I changed the passage? Worst of all, have I changed the passage to suit my tastes and thoughts?

It is a difficult question. It is some time since I have realized that giving the Torah voice has also changed my ears. I hear Torah differently. I find vividness of character portrayal, complexity of action, and a sophisticated and wise moral perspective in every reading. In the next Chapter, after discussing in more detail how the chant works for me, I will offer two examples from Genesis of stories that were opened to me by the chant. Without chant, the richness — literary and spiritual — of Scripture is often missed. Orthodox believers and homiletic teachers run the risk of diminishing Torah by transmuting its subtle shadings into black and white lessons. Modernists can be guilty of temporal chauvinism, and miss the depth, complexity and wisdom because they view Torah as the all-too-human product of a more primitive time. But the depths of Torah are preserved in the music of the chant. The *ba'al keri'ah*'s job is to make this evident to the listener.

It is deplorable that the literature of the ballad has attracted so much more attention than the music. The two elements should never be disassociated. The music and text are one and indivisible, and to sever one from the other is to remove the priceless gem from its beautiful setting.

Lead character Lily Penleric
Quoted in the movie *Songcatcher*,
by Maggie Greenwald

Chapter 4
The Workings of Chant

HOW DOES ONE LEARN TO SING the Torah? It is not difficult to learn the basics. I have watched several generations of students in our synagogue become Torah readers with only a few weeks of training, guided by any of several skillful teachers. Here is how the process works.

Each "note," or trop/*ta'am,* in the chant is a musical phrase with its own symbol and name. The notes can be linked into longer musical phrases, and applied to a verse. The student learns to sing the variety of musical phrases from a table, and then practices applying the combinations they have learned to the text. Here is an illustration of such a table that I have borrowed from the teachers in my own synagogue.

Trope - Taamim

① מַהְפַּ֤ךְ פַּשְׁטָא֙ מֻנַּ֣ח זָקֵף־קָטֹ֔ן

② מֵרְכָ֖א טִפְחָ֖א מֻנַּ֣ח אֶתְנַחְתָּ֑א

③ מֵרְכָ֖א טִפְחָ֖א מֵרְכָ֖א סוֹף־פָּסֽוּק׃

④ קַדְמָ֨א וְאַזְלָ֜א

⑤ מֻנַּ֣ח ׀ מֻנַּ֣ח רְבִיעִ֗י

⑥ מֻנַּ֣ח זַרְקָ֮א מֻנַּ֣ח סֶגּוֹל֒

⑦ דַּרְגָּ֧א תְּבִ֛יר   מֵרְכָ֥א תְּבִ֛יר

⑧ תְּלִישָׁא־קְטַנָּ֩ה   תְּלִישָׁא־גְדוֹלָ֖ה

⑨ גֵּרְשַׁ֞יִם זָקֵף־גָּד֕וֹל אַזְלָא־גֵּ֜רֶשׁ פָּזֵ֡ר

⑩ יְתִ֚יב מֻנַּ֣ח זָקֵף־קָטֹ֔ן

I learned trop from a similar "table," the traditional "Zarka Table" found in many a *Chumash*, and used to teach students for centuries. It derives its name from the first **stop** trop on the list, **zarka**:

שְׁמוֹת הַטְּעָמִים

קַדְמָא֨ מֻנַּ֣ח זַרְקָא֮ מֻנַּ֣ח סֶגּ֒ל מֻנַּ֣ח ׀ מֻנַּ֣ח רְבִיעִ֗י
מַהְפַּ֤ךְ פַּשְׁטָא֙ מֻנַּ֣ח זָקֵף־קָטֹ֔ן זָקֵף־גָּד֕וֹל
מֵרְכָ֥א טִפְחָ֖א מֻנַּ֣ח אֶתְנַחְתָּ֑א פָּזֵ֡ר תְּלִישָׁא־
קְטַנָּ֩ה תְּלִישָׁא־גְדֹלָ֖ה קַדְמָ֨א וְאַזְלָ֜א אַזְלָא־
גֵּרֶשׁ גֵּרְשַׁ֞יִם דַּרְגָּ֧א תְּבִ֛יר יְתִ֚יב פְּסִיק ׀
סוֹף־פָּסֽוּק׃ שַׁלְשֶׁ֓לֶת קַרְנֵי־פָרָ֟ה מֵרְכָ֖א־
כְפוּלָ֦ה יֶרַח־בֶּן־יוֹמֽוֹ׃

When one has mastered all the trop, and become facile with applying it to text, one runs into the next problem. Torah read in public is in the ancient form of a scroll, written by hand, on parchment, in beautiful calligraphy. The scrolls are beautiful, and have not substantially changed for two millennia. But the scrolls lack two things necessary for an accurate authentic reading: vowels and trop. The books available to a congregation for following a reading, by contrast, have both of these later Masoretic additions. To prepare a public reading, the Torah reader uses a book called a *Tikkun*. In a *Tikkun*, each page is split vertically in two, the right hand column featuring text with vowels and trop, and the left text as it appears in the scrolls.

162	במדבר ח בהעלותך	קסב

שתים זהב כפת הקדש בשקל מאות וארבע	שְׁתֵּ֣ים זָהָ֤ב כַּפּֽוֹת הַקֹּ֔דֶשׁ בְּשֶׁ֖קֶל מֵאוֹת֙ וְאַרְבַּ֣ע
בשקל הכף עשרה קטרת מלאת עשרה	בְּשֶׁ֖קֶל הַכַּ֥ף עֲשָׂרָ֛ה קְטֹ֧רֶת מְלֵאָ֨ה עֲשָׂרָ֜ה
הבקר כל ומאה עשרים הכפות זהב כל הקדש	הַקֹּ֑דֶשׁ כָּל־זְהַ֤ב הַכַּפּוֹת֙ עֶשְׂרִ֣ים וּמֵאָ֔ה כָּל־הַבָּקָ֣ר
עשר שנים אילם פרים עשר שנים לעלה	לְעֹלָ֞ה שְׁנֵ֧ים עָשָׂ֛ר פָּרִ֖ים אֵילִ֣ם שְׁנֵים־עָשָׂ֑ר
ושעירי ומנחתם עשר שנים שנה בני כבשים	כְּבָשִׂ֤ים בְּנֵֽי־שָׁנָה֙ שְׁנֵ֣ים עָשָׂ֔ר וּמִנְחָתָ֑ם וּשְׂעִירֵ֥י
העלמים זבח וכל לחטאת עשר שנים עזים	עִזִּ֛ים שְׁנֵ֥ים עָשָׂ֖ר לְחַטָּֽאת׃ וְכֹ֞ל בְּקַ֣ר ׀ זֶ֣בַח הַשְּׁלָמִ֗ים
עתדים ששים אילם פרים וארבעה עשרים	עֶשְׂרִ֣ים וְאַרְבָּעָ֔ה פָּרִ֖ים אֵילִ֣ם שִׁשִּׁ֛ים עַתֻּדִ֥ים
המזבח חנכת זאת עושים שנה בני כבשים ששים	שִׁשִּׁ֖ים כְּבָשִׂ֣ים בְּנֵֽי־שָׁנָ֣ה שִׁשִּׁ֑ים זֹ֚את חֲנֻכַּ֣ת הַמִּזְבֵּ֔חַ
מועד אהל אל משה ובבא אתו המשוח אחרי	אַחֲרֵ֖י הִמָּשַׁ֣ח אֹת֑וֹ׃ וּבְבֹ֨א מֹשֶׁ֜ה אֶל־אֹ֣הֶל מוֹעֵד֮
אליו מדבר הקול את וישמע אתו לדבר	לְדַבֵּ֣ר אִתּוֹ֒ וַיִּשְׁמַ֨ע אֶת־הַקּ֜וֹל מִדַּבֵּ֣ר אֵלָ֗יו
הכרבים שני מבין העדת ארן על אשר הכפרת מעל	מֵעַ֨ל הַכַּפֹּ֜רֶת אֲשֶׁ֤ר עַל־אֲרֹ֣ן הָעֵדֻ֔ת מִבֵּ֖ין שְׁנֵ֣י הַכְּרֻבִ֑ים
אליו וידבר	וַיְדַבֵּ֖ר אֵלָֽיו׃

A *ba'al keri'ah* will study a portion using the right side text. Once this is committed to memory, he/she can try the left side version, referring back to the *te'amim* and vowels on the right as needed.

Although I learned trop from the Zarka Table, that system of organization is no longer the manner in which I perceive trop. I realized long ago that *Te'amei Hamikra* had sorted themselves in my mind into two melodic lines. I call them:

49

1. The Basic Rhythm

   Mahpach pashta munach zakef-katon, mercha tipcha
   munach etnachta;

   mahpach pashta munach zakef, mercha tipcha
   mercha siluk.

2. The Basic Flourish

   Pazer telisha ketana kadma ve'azla, munach [legarmeh]
   munach revi'a

1 . מַהְפָּךְ פַּשְׁטָא֙ מוּנָ֣ח זָקֵף־קָטֹ֔ן

מֵרְכָ֥א טִפְחָ֖א מוּנָ֣ח אֶתְנַחְתָּ֑א

2 . פָּזֵ֡ר תְּלִישָׁא־קְטַנָּ֩ה קַדְמָ֨א וְאַזְלָ֝א

מוּנָ֣חו מוּנָ֣ח רְבִיעִ֗י

To hear these as flowing music with a pulsating beat is to hear the music
of the Scriptures. It is also possible to break off pieces of these lines to suit
the needs of shorter verses and phrases.

The Basic Rhythm can be thought of as the pulse and beat of the Scripture,
emphasizing its underlying parallel structure. This is most clearly heard in
poetic passages, such as the Song of Moses, Deuteronomy 32. The Basic
Flourish has a beautiful sweeping melody, well suited to accentuation
and dramatization. The different *te'amim* of the Basic Flourish can also
be used individually or in smaller subgroups, interrupting and changing
the flow of the Basic Rhythm. The Basic Rhythm is well adapted for
poetic passages, but the more complex structure of prose has different
requirements. Adding the *te'amim* of the Basic Flourish lets melody
indicate punctuation, inflection and emphasis, and allows for complex
irregular sentences.

As an example of melody coloring text, consider **revi'a**, the last *ta'am* of the Basic Flourish, by way of a contemporary analogy. Many contemporary songs begin with a time word. The Beatles' "Yesterday," "Tomorrow" from the musical *Annie*, "Today" from *The Fantasticks*, "Tonight" from *West Side Story* are examples. There is a common thread to the music for the "time-word" that is both the title and first word in these songs. The melody lingers on the initial word, prolonging it, and focusing attention on the particular span of time. The musical line then takes off and flows with the description of what has happened or what is about to happen. The effect is emphasis of a time fraught with emotional meaning: yearning, nostalgia, or anticipation.

This device of musically prolonging an introductory time-word is apparently time-honored. Consider these biblical examples:

- (Genesis 44:33): "*And now*, let your servant stay instead of the lad as a slave to my lord, and let the lad go up with his brothers."

- (Exodus 16:9) And Moses said to Joshua, "Pick us out men, and go out and battle Amalek; *tomorrow*, I will stand on the hilltop, God's staff in my hand."

- (Exodus 13:29) *And it was, in the middle of the night* — and God struck down every firstborn in the land of Egypt…

The trop on each of these phrases is **revi'a**. Its name is an Aramaic word meaning "settling down to rest," a suitable description of its downward, cascading, prolonged melody. It is the trop I would choose to open the song "Yesterday" if I were doing it in biblical chant. By holding the initial time word, chant transforms the idea of settling in into direct experience, dramatizing and accentuating the significance of the moment.

- In the first example Joseph confronts his brothers for the last time in disguise as ruler of Egypt, second only to Pharaoh. Judah gives a moving description of the tight bond between father Jacob and his youngest son, Benjamin, whom Joseph has claimed as slave. It is an eloquent, moving speech, designed to transport the listener back to the tent of the elderly patriarch in Canaan. "And now" recalls us abruptly to the here and now, a sudden transition from Jacob's house to Joseph's palace and the intensity of the brothers' predicament.

- The second example occurs during another tense moment. Israel has just made it across the Red Sea, only to be beset by enemies in the desert. For the first time they have to battle on their own behalf. Joshua is to assemble an army and go out to do battle, but it is clear that the people will still need divine help. Musically holding "tomorrow" is a means of emphasizing this critical need, a reassuring and hopeful word. Tomorrow, as for Annie, will be different.

- Finally, at the dramatic climax of the story of the ten plagues, **revi'a** prolongs the momentous "And it was, in the middle of the night…" evoking suspense and mystery.

But trop does more than add emphasis, depth, and nuance to single words. It also taps into ancient and deep strata of meaning in the text that may have been buried under layers of commentary and scholarship. I will offer two more examples from Genesis of how trop has led me to alternative readings of familiar stories, different from their usual spin. Let's examine the story of Isaac's birth to see how the trop leads to a richer and more emotionally complex take on familiar tales.

The Birth of Isaac: Laughter and a musical joke

The story of Isaac, whose name *Yitzchak* in Hebrew means "he will laugh," has served as one of my principle reminders that the music of chant helps to hear the text fully. There is a layer of simple meaning, *p'shat* as we call it, which is richer than commonly recognized, and reaches the highest level of literary purpose. There are occasions when a long-accepted reading of the text has become so ingrained that it becomes almost a barrier to listening to the words of Scriptures. A singular trop, on a single verse in this story, suggests a variant, simpler reading of the text.

Isaac's birth is foretold to Abraham at the opening of *Parashat Vayera* (Genesis 18). *Vayera* tells of three "men" appearing to Abraham and the hospitality with which he greets them. Soon, these three men will reveal themselves to be angelic messengers of God. While dining under a tree, they tell the aged Abraham that his ninety-year-old wife Sarah will give birth to a son at the same season in the next year. Sarah, standing at the tent flap, overhears and laughs inwardly: "After being shriveled shall I have youthful pleasure? And my husband is old." God[18] asks Abraham why she laughed and seems to criticize Sarah for lack of belief: "Is anything too wondrous for God?" Sarah, afraid, denies having laughed. But the angel has the last word: "No, you did laugh."

The usual reading of this passage suggests that the Torah is critical of Sarah, that her laughter betrays skepticism. She has committed an error, or worse, a sin, and God rebukes her. Tradition contrasts her doubts with Abraham's quiet acceptance, indicating his complete faith in God's word, however improbable. This interpretation endures to this day. Art Scroll: "Although Sarah did not know this truly was a message from God Himself, God was angered at her reaction, for a person of her great stature should have had faith that the miracle of birth *could* happen." *Etz Hayim* comments, "The Bible does not gloss over the failings of Israel's traditional heroes."

But this commonly held understanding of the story does not entirely make sense. In our scenario, Sarah is listening to three men dining with her husband, who have yet to reveal their angelic nature. Why would incredulity be taken as deserving criticism? Also notable is that Sarah laughed at all. Infertility is the great tragedy of her life. Her alternate plan to have an adoptive son via her handmaiden Hagar has gone terribly amiss, and has been a source of torment rather than satisfaction. How can she laugh at all, even with bitterness, as some commentators suggest? I will revisit these questions after a broader look at comedy and laughter in the birth of Isaac.

---

[18] "The greatest angel among them" — Rashbam. "Apparently one of the men, angels of God" — Casuto.

The Hebrew Scriptures are notable for moments of humor. Comedy involves a sympathetic understanding of humans and their foibles. As amply illustrated in many literary examples from speeches to political satire, comedy can have a serious purpose and an important message. I am not saying that the Torah is frivolous, but rather the opposite. It is not plausible that this work, which is characterized throughout with what Alter has called a "serious playfulness" would miss employing the device of comedy, so long a part of the storyteller's craft, in making its point and reaching to the heart.[19]

It is not surprising to find humor in the account of the birth of one named "he will laugh." In the account of the birth of Isaac, laughter is pure laughter — the laughter of enjoyment, mirth, and explosive gladness; the laughter of joyful surprise. The darker side of the story is dramatic irony. We the readers are aware of the destiny of this family. There will be a schism, and much to his chagrin, Abraham will have to expel his firstborn son, Ishmael. Isaac will come perilously close to becoming a sacrifice. Like episodes of comic relief in a serious drama, the tale of Isaac's birth is a joyous interlude in an otherwise complex tale. It was trop that called this to my attention. The use of laughter in the episode at Abraham's tent is better understood by looking at the entire story. Chapter 18 is not the first time that the hundred-year-old Abraham

---

[19] Other examples include: (1) Exodus 14:11: the people Israel to Moses at the Red Sea, Pharaoh bearing down on them (sarcastically): "Are there no graves in Egypt?" (2) Genesis 31 includes a "Tevya-Golda" moment when Jacob nervously prepares Rachel and Leah for leaving their father's house, clearly worried how they will take his machinations, only to discover that they are far ahead of him in their assessment of their father's duplicity. Later in the same story a tense moment in the Laban-Jacob encounter is broken up when Rachel tells her father that she can't arise from the camel's saddle in which she has hidden his idols because she is on her period. (3) Many stories from Judges employ grim humor. For example (Judges 3), the hero Ehud makes his getaway after stabbing the obese tyrant Eglon, the knife disappearing into layers of abdominal fat. Eglon soils himself, and his courtiers presume he is using the toilet. Ehud makes his escape as they hesitate to intrude. (4) Samuel I 25:22: the fugitive David swears that he will not leave alive "one wall-pisser" of Naval's house (in case anyone wondered why some translators render "one male" and others "one dog.") He must have been pretty mad.

is told he will have a son by his ninety-year-old postmenopausal wife, Sarah. The first such pledge is in Chapter 17, read the previous week at the end of *Parashat Lech Lecha*. The trop in this portion includes a musical joke that directs how the passage is to be read.

As Genesis 17 begins, Abraham is far along in years. In exchange for following God's instructions, he had made a covenant with God, who promised a special destiny for his descendants. As he grew older without any progeny, his wife Sarah had persuaded him to have a child by her handmaiden, Hagar. Ishmael was born of this union, but the rivalry which developed between the two women as a result of this pregnancy proved an ongoing torment to the household. Thirteen years have passed without major event, when (Genesis 17:1) God again speaks to Abraham. He renews the covenant and specifies circumcision of all males as its sign. Then God makes a surprising promise (Genesis 17: 15-21)

> And God said to Abraham, "Sarai your wife shall no longer call her name Sarai, for Sarah is her name. And I will bless her and I will also give you from her a son; and I will bless him and she shall become nations, kings of peoples shall issue from her." And Abraham fell on his face[20] laughing; and he said to himself,
>
> "To a hundred year old man will a child be born?
>
> And Sarah — will a ninety year old woman give birth?"
>
> And Abraham said to God, "Would that Ishmael might live in your favor."

---

[20] I have taken the liberty of translating this phrase literally. Alter renders "flung himself on his face, and he laughed;" others "prostrated himself" to indicate a more voluntary, controlled act. "Falling on one's face" is an act of obeisance, and Abraham does this also earlier in the passage (verse 3), when God first reveals his covenantal intent. It has been interpreted as a sign of awe (Rashi), thanks (Casuto), or as prostration preparatory to prayer. Any or all of these fit the passage. But the Hebrew root *nf'l* also fits involuntary falling, so I propose the image of Abraham falling down helplessly with laughter as he prostrates himself.

And God said, "But — *Sarah your wife* is to bear you a son, and you shall call his name Isaac [*Yitz'chak* — he will laugh]; and I will establish my covenant with him as an everlasting covenant, and for his seed after him. And as for Ishmael, I have heard you. Here, I will bless him and make him fruitful, and will multiply him most abundantly; twelve chieftains he will beget, and I will make him a great nation. But my covenant I will establish with Isaac, whom Sarah will bear you at this season next year."

I first noticed the humor in this passage because of the chant. Musical jokes work by means of the same mechanism as do many jokes: start a line so listeners are expecting one sort of completion of a phrase or theme, and then suddenly change direction in a surprising fashion. The effect is not necessarily humorous. Surprise can be jarring, frightening. A humorous effect will depend also on the milieu of the phrase. It is the combination of surprise and context that will make for humor.

The simple sense of the story is that God's announcement had struck Abraham as so comical that he falls down laughing. When he recovers he asks for Ishmael's welfare, as if saying, "You almost got me there, God, but really I would be content if you look after Ishmael." The text then reads:

> *Vayomer Elohim, "Aval Sarah ishtecha yoledet lecha ben ...*
> And said God, "But Sarah your wife is to bear to you a son
>
> **munach revi'a pashta munach revi'a mahpach pashta zakef**

The *te'amim* will hint to us that this is said humorously, in line with the tone of the rest of the passage. The above sequence is an example of highly unusual, and even "incorrect" trop. Coming after the first **pashta, munach revi'a** is unexpected, a "forbidden" or certainly unusual trop sequence.[21] **Pashta munach revi'a** is a sudden change of direction. It is

---

[21] Plaut, *The Torah: A Modern Commentary*, p. 133. More "normal" sequence could be **pashta munach zakef** or **legarmeh munach revi'a** for example. These sequences do not punctuate the verse correctly, but are common trop sequences. We also find **pashta munach revi'a** in the tale of Isaac's blessing (Gen 27:37), perhaps

a humorous effect. God continues in a joshing manner: "But — Sarah your wife! She will bear you a son. And yes, it is funny. In fact, name him 'he will laugh!'." In other words, trop suggests that Abraham's first reaction, like Sarah's later, is laughter *and* incredulity.

Classical *Midrash*[22] sometimes reads this passage differently. It takes Abraham's concern for Ishmael to reflect a sense of concern that Ishmael may lose God's protection: "Now that Sarah is about to bear my heir, please do not abandon Ishmael." Tradition tells us that Abraham's laughter in his "heart" [*belibo*] is the laughter of pleasure in the fulfillment of God's promise, while Sarah's laughing "inwardly" [*bekirbah*] reflects her disbelief that her atrophic uterus will bear a child. This view fits with the canonic figure of Abraham, exemplar of the man of faith. But the Abraham of Genesis 17 is a more human character, and his laughter reflects a sense of surprise that is readily understandable, *even in one whose faith is strong*. This is clear in the text as well. God's response to Abraham is not: *"Yes*, I will take care of Ishmael too." Rather it is, "*But*, Sarah your wife will bear you a son…." The introductory "but" makes sense only if Abraham's request is counter to the possibility that Sarah could conceive. Both Abraham and Sarah react to the announcement with incredulous laughter. While one can reach this perspective through a close and careful reading of the text, the chant will call it to attention in a clear — and humorous — fashion.

I return to my earlier questions about the second story of the foretelling of the birth of Isaac in Chapter 18. Why would Sarah's incredulity be deserving of criticism? How can a barren, elderly woman laugh at all? Torah insists on the convention of describing speech and action, not mood or thought. So we are left to guess Sarah's internal state. It is not hard for me to imagine that Sarah's laughter signals she has at least partially accepted her barren state. She can treat a completely absurd

---

also in the vein of an unexpected twist which alters Isaac's intentions for the destiny of his two children, and perhaps a musical reference to the manner in which Isaac's birth changed Abraham's expectations for his firstborn, Ishmael. As we shall see further in Leviticus, Torah is capable of just such complicated musical references.

[22] See Rashi, who quotes the Midrash.

comment overheard at the dinner table with laughter, an indication of surprise. The angel's rebuke "Is anything too wondrous for God?" is not scolding but playful teasing. Sarah's fearful reply is understandable — she suddenly realizes that she is in the presence of the supernatural, and that these are not ordinary men. I would even read the last line, "No, you laughed," as indicating, "No, you did laugh, but it's OK." Were I a director, I would play this scene as comical, without changing a line!

The Torah picks up the narrative a year after the announcement of the three angels, when the promise comes to fruition. Sarah's joy again overflows and expresses itself in laughter:

> "Laughter has God made for me,
> Whoever hears will laugh for me."
>
> And she said
>
> "Who would have uttered to Abraham —
>
> 'Sarah is suckling sons!'
>
> For I have borne a son for his old age."
>
> And the child grew up and was weaned. And Abraham made a great feast on the day Isaac was weaned.

Even in translation the surprising, exuberant joy that we call laughter jumps off the page. I read this verse with a chuckle in my voice when I chant it in shul.

The process of *Midrash* represents a two thousand year conversation with our sacred texts. It is not merely the process by which we come to know Scripture; it is also a means for understanding ourselves, the world around us, and our place in it. Trop is one more access point for interpretation, and an important one. Our traditions sometimes provide us with archetypal figures giving a univocal response to a situation. Thus the image of a trusting Abraham whose faith is contrasted with Sarah's doubts, has been handed down for generations and become fixed in our minds. The musical reading transforms the figures we encounter from mythic, larger-than-life heroes to human characters who, with all their greatness, display human foibles and understandable reactions. This is in accord with the Genesis narrative. Manly strength contrasted with female weakness is not the theme of this story. Throughout Genesis, women's intuition about the destiny of their children carries Divine endorsement. The relationships in Genesis are life partnerships, with each partner having a critical role to play in the future of the clan.

Abraham argues with God: the art of storytelling

It is easy to miss the deft narrative touches that transform biblical stories from fables with morals into rich literary narratives — dramas with fully conceived characters, and plots full of surprise, humor and pathos. A close look at a familiar story, Abraham's pleading with God over the fate of Sodom and Gomorrah, can serve as another example of how the music of chant can impact how we hear Torah.

After the announcement of the birth of Isaac, two of the three angels continue on their mission to the cities of the plain. The story of Abraham's argument with God over the fate of Sodom and Gomorrah in Genesis 18 is familiar. The dialogue revolves around arithmetical points: just how many righteous people are needed to save a city? Commentators and theologians have discussed this passage over the ages, elaborating on its complex moral concepts. For example, Gunther Plaut[23] writes: "God's ways are ultimately 'past finding out,' but this does not prevent man from trying to bring them as much as possible within his own horizon of understanding. And this horizon is not, in Abraham's case, limited by tribal considerations. His is a universal concept of justice…. He is a man for all men."

I could have chosen any number of other commentators. The focus is typically on homiletical and philosophical lessons to be drawn from this story. We tend to lose Abraham the person, and he becomes a representative of Humanity or of the Jewish tradition. What is missing? When we call out the passage in chant, we add the richness of storytelling

---

[23] Plaut, *The Torah: A Modern Commentary*, p. 133.

— drama, psychological depth, empathetic understanding. An unusual trop pattern calls attention to the complex depiction of the scene and to its dramatization as an encounter between vast and small.

In Genesis 18: 18-19, God meditates on the need to inform Abraham, whose descendants will be expected to set an example for just behavior, of the impending destruction of the twin cities of the plain, Sodom and Gomorrah. How could his descendants fulfill their mission to be just and charitable, if they did not see God as just and right? Their perspective is to be radically different from the worldview of surrounding peoples, who experienced natural forces embodied by the gods as whimsical and cruel. The concept of a just and loving Creator in place of capricious gods lies at the heart of the difference between the monotheistic and pagan outlook. God hints his intent to Abraham, and the latter objects on precisely this basis: "Far be it from you! Will the judge of all the earth not do justice?" There follows a long exchange, in which Abraham bargains down the number of innocent/righteous people needed for God to spare the doomed cities from fifty individuals to ten. Alter comments on the imbalance of the passage — Abraham wordy and elaborate, God's responses terse and to the point:[24]

> Here, Abraham, aware that he is walking a dangerous tight rope … deploys a whole panoply of the abundant rhetorical devices of ancient Hebrew for expressing self-abasement before a powerful figure. At each turn of the dialogue, God responds only by stating flatly that He will not destroy for the sake of the number of innocent just stipulated. The dialogue is cast very much as a bargaining exchange…. Each time he ratchets down the number he holds back the new, smaller number, in good bargaining fashion to the very end of this statement.

The trop in this passage calls attention to this quality of chutzpah — a creature as small, fleeting, and frail as a human challenging the Master of all creation. Trop called my attention to the psychological realism of the dialogue, and led me to reexamine the story as scripted drama. The trop

---

[24] Alter, *The Five Books*

that first caught my notice was a thrice-repeated musical phrase from the Basic Flourish — **telisha gershayim** (**TG**) — that introduces Abraham's remarks in verses 28, 30, and 32. These are not rare trop, but they caught my ear. It is unusual to run across this combination several times in rapid succession. There are many other ways these verses could have been accented, besides this fairly interesting combination. Their effect musically is one of quaking hesitation, of a tentative approach, consistent with Alter's observation that Abraham is "aware that he is walking a dangerous tight rope" in addressing God. Verses 23-33:

> And Abraham stepped forward and said: "Will you really [*ha'af*] wipe out righteous with wicked? Perhaps there are fifty righteous within the city; will you really wipe out and not spare the place, for the sake of the fifty righteous within it? Far be it from you to do such a thing, to put to death righteous with wicked; and the righteous will be just like the wicked. Far be it from you! Will the judge of all the earth not do justice?"

> And God said: "If I find in Sodom fifty righteous in the midst of the city, I will spare the whole place for their sake."

> And Abraham came forward and said: "Here now, I've presumed to speak to my Lord, and I am dust and ashes. *Perhaps there will be lacking* (**TG**) five from the fifty virtuous people; would you destroy the whole city for the five?"

> And He said, [25] "I will not destroy if I find there forty five."

---

[25] The inconsistent punctuation of the quotative frame ("and he said") is meant to convey a taste of the way trop plays with the rhythm of voiced speech in its complicated grammar. With four levels of pauses, trop can imitate a range of speech, from rapid-fire staccato to a more deliberate response. In this schema, I have indicated level 1 and 2 **stops** and the "strong" level 3 **revi'a** with a semicolon, and other level 3 and level 4 **stops** with the lesser commas. If you also imagine the more drawn out music of the level 4 **telisha** on the last two italicized quotes, the chant depiction is yet subtler. It is a musical, syncopated accentuation of Abraham's wordy and elaborate pleas, contrasting with God's terse replies.

And he went on to speak to him and said: "Perhaps there will be found there forty."

And He said, "I won't do it for the sake of the forty."

And he said, "May my Lord not (**TG**) be angry, and let me speak; perhaps there will be found thirty."

And He said, "I won't do it if I find there thirty."

And he said: "Here now I have presumed to speak to my Lord. Perhaps there will be found twenty."

And he said, "I will not destroy for the sake of the twenty."

And he said, "May the Lord not (**TG**) be angry and I will speak one last time. Perhaps there will be found there ten.

And He said, "I will not destroy for the sake of the ten."

And God went off, when He had finished speaking to Abraham; and Abraham returned to his place.

The music of the phrases I have highlighted with italics is in accord with Abraham's hesitant language of exaggerated courtly politeness. The trop also makes it easier to hear a detail that Alter did not comment upon. Abraham's polite tone is a sudden change. His initial reaction had been bold and impertinent.

Abraham's change from outrage to polite pleading makes even more sense if we reexamine the beginning of the story. God's initial address to Abraham is oblique. He avoids spelling out precisely what is about to happen. It is a strangely tentative approach by the Master of the Universe, and says several things about the relationship of God to his chosen emissary. He is uncertain about how Abraham might respond, and also cares about his reaction (v.20):

How great the outcry of Sodom and Gomorrah; how very heavy has their sin grown.

Let me go down, please, and see whether, like the outcry that comes to me, they have dealt destruction; and if not, I shall know.

God does not actually tell Abraham what He is about to do. Torah portrays the Divine/human encounter through the metaphor of human relationships. Above, in the story of the birth of Isaac, there was a kidding tone in the exchange between God and Abraham. In the story of Sodom and Gomorrah the Creator, concerned that His acts will be misinterpreted, sensitively broaches the issue in a roundabout way. The language is unclear and elusive. The inclusion of the word "please" indicates he is asking for approval. The tone is similar to how husband might approach wife in a tentative manner, suspecting she will have no part in upcoming plans, once she hears of them.

Abraham holds back for a minute, and two angelic visitors leave. When Abraham and God are alone, however, he does not contain his outrage about the threat that he sees clearly despite God's indirection (v.23-25). As one who knows his partner well, Abraham can read more in what God does not say, and in the diffident nature of the approach, than is said in the words. Abraham's response is immediate, and harshly critical of God's unspoken intentions. This first address is audacious, almost rude. Only after God's acceptance of Abraham's logic and terms does the human realize the brazen tone of his speech. Perhaps his eyes are suddenly open and he realizes, to use Alter's metaphor, that he is like a man on a tight rope who has just looked down. The **telisha gershayim** trop in Abraham's speech strikes an immediately hesitant note that should be as plain as any commentary or stage direction in indicating the change.

Why this story? God's purpose, the Torah's mission statement, is indicated in His reflection prior to informing Abraham of the coming destruction:

Am I concealing from Abraham what I am about to do? And Abraham — he *will* become a great and mighty nation, and all the nations of the earth will be blessed through him. For I have chosen [lit. known][26] him, so that he will command his sons and household after him, and they will keep the way of God to do righteousness and justice (*tzedakah* and *mishpat*); in order for God to bring upon Abraham what He spoke about him[27].

This is the first time Scripture confronts a question that it will raise repeatedly, if indirectly, in many contexts: How can a powerful and merciful God allow suffering and destruction to happen? If God is often the direct cause of calamities, how can these events be reconciled with the notion of a just and even compassionate God? There has never been a satisfactory, logically consistent answer to these questions. The problem of Evil was never solved by philosophy. But for the Jewish people these are not casual questions or mental exercise. At the heart of the monotheistic vision lies the conviction that God is just and merciful. The survival of the Jewish people and its religion has depended on being able to look national tragedy in the face and still proclaim their adherence to God and to His law.

Like Abraham, we need to feel comfortable with the order of the universe, even if our first reaction is outrage at the way things happen. A fully consistent, reasoned explanation is impossible. The philosopher's "problem of evil" cannot be resolved with pure logic. We seek resolution on a psychological level, and that is one of the reasons we tell ourselves stories. Myth and story are means of grappling with ambiguous, enigmatic and complex issues in order to come to a personal resolution.

Abraham's plea is the Torah's first attempt to come to terms with this issue and is not the final one. There is a progression from Noah to Abraham to Moses. Noah hears the world will be destroyed and builds ın ark to save his family. Abraham argues with God about the justice of

---

[26] The word *yeda'tiv* is the identical word that is used to indicate intimacy between and wife.

d told Abraham (Genesis 12:1-3): "…And I will make you into a great will bless you, … and all the families of the earth will be blessed destroying Sodom, but is ultimately placated when he is reassured that God will spare the city for the sake of even ten upright citizens. Abraham is occupied entirely with *mishpat*, Justice. Moses is the ultimate human partner God seeks. After the episode of the golden calf he recognizes that Israelites, whom God proposes to annihilate, are without merit. He nevertheless pleads for God's mercy. Justice tempered by the quality of compassion is the ultimate goal of God, and its proclamation is the mission of the Jewish people, as already foreshadowed in our story here in Genesis.

I would not have heard the story of Abraham's argument with God in its fullness without attending to it in chant. I might have missed the transition from moral outrage to hesitant bargaining. I might not have noticed the intimate touches, which imply that God himself is like a nervous suitor in approaching His creatures. The tale gains richness, psychological texture, and emotional force if perceived as a literary narrative rather than as a fable about a larger than life mythological figure who holds even God to a standard of just behavior. It becomes a fully realized story and not a philosophical concept or a simple allegory. And stories are the ways humans learn about life with both intellectual and emotional understanding.

Such is the landscape that I have come to inhabit as a Torah reader. Chant has been the magical doorway leading into it, and exploring its paths has been a great source of pleasure. But one must be careful. The Jewish way is to balance love and passion with caution and logical thought. Ardor is to be tempered by reverence. Had the process of learning and writing about chant uncovered additional layers of richness in the Genesis stories, *dayenu* — it would have been enough for me! But there was a greater surprise in store for me when I came upon a full-blown narrative story in the heart of Leviticus, a book that seems occupied only with priestly ritual. This story too is not a simple legend, but a fine example of the intricate plot and character portrayal seen in the best literature. It too is concerned in a sophisticated and sensitive manner with the question of human suffering. Tucked away in Leviticus, the story of the death of Aaron's sons, Nadav and Avihu, has been hidden from full view for millennia. Like the Abraham stories, it revealed its inner secrets in its trop. The tale of this discovery occupies the second part of this book.

PART TWO
YIR'AH — FEAR

Light up our eyes with your Torah, and cause our hearts to
stick to your commandments, and *unite our hearts* to love and
fear you, and we will never be ashamed.

Daily Prayerbook, before "Shema Yisrael…"

Once [Reb] Zusya prayed to God: "Lord, I love you so
much, but I do not fear you enough! Let me stand in awe
of you like your angels, who are penetrated by your awe-
inspiring name." And God heard his prayer and His name
penetrated the hidden heart of Zusya as it does those of
the Angels. But Zusya crawled under the bed like a little
dog and animal fear shook him until he howled, "Lord, let
me love you like Zusya again." And God heard him this
time also.

Martin Buber, *Tales of the Hasidim*

Chapter 5
Te'amei Hamikra — Song or Grammar?

IF TORAH IS SONG, THEN WE HAVE AN
obligation to proceed with caution. Music sweeps us off our feet and gets
us dancing. If we are not careful, we can find ourselves following a pied
piper to an unknown destination. *Ahavah* — love/enthusiasm — must
be tempered with *yir'ah* — fear/awe/caution. We pray not for love to
conquer fear, but for the right balance of these two sides of our selves.
We wish them to be integrated together in the proper balance in our
hearts. In Part One of this book, I talked of the sensual and literary

pleasure of hearing the Torah in chant, and how it augments the power of the Torah's words. I advocated for an experience of Torah in its weekly public readings that is direct, powerful, moving, and pleasurable. It should be a high spiritual moment. In such a moment, insight and revelation are possible. Part Two of this book will examine whether or not, and to what degree, such spontaneous individual insights are valid and desirable. Earlier chapters dealt with relatively familiar stories from Genesis. Now we will take up a less known story from the heart of the Torah, focusing particularly on musical interpretation. This will lead to a fresh look at the Torah's artistry and the complexity of its thought in its explorations of God, the world, and Israel's mission.

Chant reinforces and amplifies the obvious emotional effects of the Torah's stories. It transforms dry material such as lists and genealogy into music and poetry. It is a wonderful doorway to the meaning of Scripture, sometimes to meaning that is easily missed. The Book of Leviticus is nearly devoid of narrative. This lack, as well as its preoccupation with sacrificial ritual, has made it difficult to penetrate. A common opinion is that Leviticus is dull and ponderous, and that only some sections are relevant to the modern experience. But in the very heart of Leviticus, Chapters 8-10, there is a hidden story. It is beautifully told, with the full power of narrative art that we expect from the Genesis stories. Like the Genesis tales, it is fraught with moral ambiguity, and touches on life's most complex concerns. This passage, and one portion of it in particular, has more unusual trop than any other in Torah. The chant has gone out of its way to call attention to the telling of the dedication of the Tabernacle in the Wilderness. "Wake up! Take notice!" it seems to be saying. This apparently ordinary ritualistic text bears much closer examination.

But first an admission: In Part One, we dealt exclusively with musical aspects of *Te'amei Hamikra* without exploring their other critically important function: trop is the grammar of the text. It provides the equivalent of our periods and commas, as well as punctuation marks even subtler than that. Joshua Jacobson in *The Art of Cantillation* (p.24) gives illustrations of how a comma can change the meaning in a verse.

To borrow one of his examples, Isaiah 40:3 begins in the King James translation: "A voice cries in the Wilderness, 'Prepare ye the way of the Lord'." This misreading may be familiar. It opens Handel's *Messiah*. The correct punctuation, according to both the Masoretic trop and the parallel structure of the verse, is: "A voice cries: 'In the wilderness, prepare the way of the Lord'." That is the way it is read it in the Haftarah portion for *Shabbat Nachamu* which begins, "Comfort ye, comfort ye my people…" In recording written chant notation, the Masoretes made sure that when the text is read today, it is with the same grammar and meaning with which it has been read over the centuries. In other words, the Masoretes were attentive to preserving not only the written version of Scripture, but also its sound when read aloud, and its precise punctuation. We cannot tell what melodies were used to chant Scriptures 1,000 years ago, but we know that they parsed and interpreted the verse in the same way. The grammar of the trop has been well worked out. It is a great aid to the *ba'al keri'ah* who wants to raise his or her skills to a higher level. The validity and value of the grammatical analysis of *Te'amei Hamikra* are beyond question.

So is trop music or grammar? The two perspectives on *Te'amei Hamikra* can be called the grammatical and the musical perspectives. The imaginary spirits advancing these contrasting views, the Grammarian and the Singer, will be introduced in a fable. Solely for the purpose of maintaining narrative clarity in the use of pronouns, I will pretend that the Grammarian is male, and the Singer female.

Ahavah and Yir'ah—*Te'amei Hamikra*: music or grammar, a fable

There is a silent debate between the Grammarian and the Singer about which of their worldviews is correct. This debate is unconscious, unspoken. Neither recognizes the disagreement. The Singer is largely unaware of the grammatical perspective. She "knows" how to punctuate the verse and breathe based on musical phrasing. She can sing the melody for the *te'amim*, she can sight-read text with *te'amim*. With time to prepare, she can make the text sing. When she has read Torah, her listeners are elated, and come away with a strong sense of the beauty and mystery of the text. Ask the Singer about conjunctives and disjunctives, and you will draw a blank. She is aware of the existence of grammatical rules of trop, but cannot tell you even the most basic of them, such as the division of **stops** into pauses of different strengths. This does not bother her, for she knows that she has gotten the verse right simply by following the musical phrasing. She rarely writes articles, let alone books. Her writings consist of short pieces, typically in a popular journal or on the Internet. She is passionate about what she does, and has a Romantic's sense of her mission to bring the text to life. The Singer is right-brained — concerned with music, emotion and large patterns. The Singer is all about *Ahavah* — love, spirit, enthusiasm.

The Grammarian is occupied with the intricacies of the rules of biblical language. He has little concern for sound, and insists that words, grammar, and syntax are the only legitimate guides to interpreting the text. His approach might threaten to take the music out of the Singer's chant, and replace it with a dry faithfulness to accuracy of pronunciation and punctuation, but for the inaccessibility of his work. The grammatical rules have little impact on the performance of the Singer, who, as I noted above, is not generally acquainted with the rules, especially not in the detail it takes to apply them. The Grammarian is vaguely annoyed at this inattention, and is aware of times that the Singer errs in her performance, which he terms "sloppy." He is a little more annoyed that the Teachers of text listen to the Singer's melody, and use it to learn insights about the texts. The Grammarian often holds an academic position. His writings will be found in scholarly journals and books. There are lots of footnotes. He is devoted to what he does, and has the scholar's passion and joy in discovery of patterns. The Grammarian is left-brained and skeptical, concerned with analysis and logically provable truth. The Grammarian is about *Yir'ah* — fear, reverence, caution, and strict faithfulness.

An interesting feature of this debate is that it is silent and unconscious. The Singer does not know that the Grammarian questions her soaring spirit. The Grammarian is aware of the Singer's rhapsody, but chooses not to call lapses of accuracy to her attention, at least not in a very effective way. He does nothing to keep the Teachers from attaching too much significance to the Singer's melodies. He sighs, and dismisses these fanciful musical interpretations as irrelevant. The Grammarian's restraint in this matter is interesting. Does it come from recognition that the grammatical edifice, for all its mathematical beauty, is not likely to be understood and appreciated by most of the listeners, the aim and target of the entire enterprise? Does he realize that his work is an analysis of the Singer's craft, a breaking off of a piece of it and discovering its logic? Does he have a sense of interdependence with the Singer, knowing that she keeps alive what he studies? Can the Grammarian answer these questions?

The Grammarian and the Singer—marriage made in heaven or irreconcilable differences?

The Grammarian and the Singer are archetypes. There is no one who is all Grammarian or all Singer. The parable which I have presented is an exaggeration, and is particularly unfair to "the grammarians," who are not ignorant of the musical origins of *te'amim* in chant. For example, Joshua Jacobson, who often takes a strictly grammatical position, is a musician. He is eloquent in his description of the music of Chant. On the other hand, this imaginary fable is useful in terms of clarity. And there is a sense in which it is fair. For while there is no one who is entirely grammarian or singer, Torah readers express one or the other tendency to varying degrees. Neither is all right or all wrong. The trick is to find the right balance, to make a marriage of the two currents. The Grammarian's position on the question of interpretation, however, does constitute a bit of a problem. It can lead the musical at heart to question their insights. It is easy to show that this fable is not entirely imaginary. There are in fact two different approaches to Trop, and at least some people, mainly "grammarians," consider these two viewpoints to be antagonistic. An example can best illustrate this. A case in point is that rare and yet familiar trop, **Shalshelet**.

Although uncommon, **Shalshelet** has a very dramatic sound and is well known to synagogue attendees. It is a rare trop, occurring only four times in the Torah, and only seven in all of Tanakh.[28] Its musical meaning has been well described and will seem obvious to a listener.[29] The Singer's viewpoint on the meaning of **Shalshelet** is well represented in the "Parashah Commentary for HayyeI Sarah," 5764 [2004], by Chancellor Ismar Schorsch of the Jewish Theological Seminary of America. He gives a description of the Masoretic accent sign and its traditional sound: "The particular mark is called a *Shalshelet* or chain. With its wiggle shape, it actually looks like a worm, always appearing above the word it serves. Its extended sound, longer than any other mark, matches its form, that is, it wavers going up and down the scale twice before finishing on a third ascent. The music connotes emotional turmoil…."

Schorsch continues with an elegant summary of the meaning of **Shalshelet** in its three occurrences in Genesis. He begins with the second instance, which occurs in *Parashat Chayyei Sarah*:

> Abraham, advanced in years and eager to arrange a marriage for his son Isaac, has sent the steward of his household back

---

[28] In this and all discussions I will use the word "*Tanakh*" to indicate the "twenty one" books of the Hebrew Scriptures, excluding the "Emet" books — Psalms, Proverbs, and Job, which have a different system of chant.

[29] Friends and lay Torah readers, hearing that I was writing about the music of Torah chant, often said to me: "Oh, you mean like **Shalshelet.**" I had originally intended to avoid discussing this trop altogether. I felt that this was an example of a *ta'am* whose dramatic import was so obvious as to not merit discussion, and that I had little to say that was worth adding. That was until I found the fourth **Shalshelet,** or rather the fourth **Shalshelet** found me. Like many, I could name two or three of the occurrences of the trop in Genesis, but where was the fourth? On the word *Vayish'chat* ("And he slaughtered") in Leviticus 8? Surely that was proof that the Grammarian is right: **Shalshelet's** presence is dictated by grammatical rules, and any interpretation based on its sound is fanciful and imaginary. Discovering the secret of the fourth **Shalshelet** left me shouting "Eureka!" and explaining my thesis to anyone who would listen.

to Mesopotamia to find a suitable mate. The narrative is full of tenderness. The steward arrives and goes to the well at which women tend to congregate. Utterly alone, he turns to the God of Abraham for help. Over the introductory word in the narrative, "*vayomar*" (and he said) appears a *Shalshelet*, conveying all the angst and trepidation felt by the steward in the face of his impossible mission (Genesis 24:12). What an inspired choice to enliven the reading!

Not surprisingly, the *Shalshelet*, which occurs but seven times in the entire Tanakh punctuates the book of Genesis. We met it last week in the rescue of Lot by the divine messengers from the doomed cities of Sodom and Gomorrah. Despite their urging, Lot is paralyzed by ambivalence: "Still he delayed. So the men seized his hand and the hands of his wife and his two daughters…" (Genesis 19:16). A *Shalshelet* is affixed to the rare verb for delaying, underlining Lot's emotional state.

And we will meet it again in the failed seduction of Joseph in Egypt by Potiphar's wife. He spurns her advances: "After a time, his master's wife cast her eyes upon Joseph and said: 'Lie with me.' But he refused…" (Genesis 39:7). The last word is unpacked with yet another *Shalshelet*, suggesting that Joseph's resolve came only after inner struggle.

Schorsch's description of the effect of **Shalshelet** on its listeners is accurate. His reading of the above passages is not new, but reflects traditions of *Midrashic* traditions going back to Mishnaic times. Rabbi Neil Gillman, comments on the weekly portion *Vayeshev*, which contains Joseph's **Shalshelet**, "The very use of this extended musical phrase is clearly meant to give us an insight into the state of mind of the personality involved. Just as the music forces us to linger, to hesitate, to feel a certain tension or ambivalence, so the person involved must be hesitant, lingering and feeling the same kind of tension or ambivalence."[30] Some experts in the grammar of *Te'amei Hamikra* acknowledge the correctness of this insight. Zechariah Goren says that **Shalshelet** "adds a certain musical

---

[30] Neil Gillman, Devar Torah, Long Island Jewish Press

dramatization to the verse." He concludes: "In any case, the intention of the *ta'am* and its *Midrash*[31] is to give psychological depth to the idea in the verse; and is an interesting attempt to peek into the emotional world of the biblical characters."[32] Surely, all can agree that this trop has obvious literary intent, that it gives an idea of what the characters are feeling, and that it highlights these passages.

Unknown to most Jewish listeners, the Grammarian takes issue with the very notion that the music of **Shalshelet** imparts valid insight into the stories in which it occurs. He would point out that **Shalshelet** always occurs on the first word of a verse, and that its usage occurs only in a verse that needs to start with a "strong" punctuation mark. The grammarians divide the trop into **connectors** and **stops**, also called **servants** and **kings**, respectively. The **connectors/kings** are divided into four levels of stops, either arranged by number (level 1 through 4) or called by a system of names (**emperors, kings, seconds,** and **thirds** is one such system; my personal favorite is **emperors, kings, officials,** and **singers**). **Shalshelet** is a **king**, or level 2 **stop**. From the point of view of the Grammarian, **Shalshelet** is rare is because it comes in a text requiring unusual punctuation.

It would be like finding a situation demanding a semicolon after the very first word or two of an English sentence. Such sentences are unusual, so there is rarely a need for **Shalshelet**. Let's listen to the nineteenth century scholar of biblical "Accentuology," William Wickes, perhaps the purest of the "Grammarians." Wickes was Christian, and doubtless not used to hearing Scriptures chanted on a regular basis. He analyzed the grammar of the Masoretic accents with no mention of their music. His passion for accurate scholarship is clearly evident, and his text remains a classic in the grammatical analysis of Scriptural chant. Wickes declares openly that the only solid, legitimate interpretation of trop is grammatical. Regarding the **Shalshelet** passages:

---

[31] i.e., that **Shalshelet** connotes emotional turmoil.

[32] Goren, "*Te'amei Hamikra Kefarshanut* (Trop as Exegisis)," p. 77.

Why, one naturally asks, a special sign for just these few (mostly unimportant) instances? There is no necessity for its introduction. For if we examine the passages and compare the rules for the exchange of **Segol** and **Zakef**,[33] we shall see that **Zakef** *might have stood in every case.* When instead of employing **Zakef**, the accentuators chose to introduce a new accent [**Shalshelet**], it must have been because they designed to attach a *special meaning* to the passages in question — to which they sought to draw attention by a particular melody and a peculiar sign. That meaning has, however, as in other similar cases, been lost. Not that the loss is a serious one. For we may be sure that we should have had some fanciful Midrash explanation, which we can well afford to dispense with [emphases are the author's].[34]

Jacobson takes an even stronger position. Contrast Schorsch's emotional and lyrical introduction of **Shalshelet** with Jacobson's first mention of this trop, an intentionally grammatical and precise formulation:

One of the characteristics of *segol* [a related trop] is that it is never found on the first word of a sentence. But in seven sentences in the "twenty-one books" there is a one-word level-two division at the beginning of the sentence that would seem to call for a *segol*. In each of these cases a different *ta'am* is substituted for *segol*. That *ta'am* is **Shalshelet**.[35]

Jacobson does not mention that this *ta'am* has a striking melody in the Ashkenazi tradition, one that will wake anyone whose attention has been drifting. He goes on to espouse the Grammarian's argument explicitly:

Some rabbis give an exegetical [interpretive] significance to this unusual *ta'am*. Their commentaries imply that the purpose of the *Shalshelet* is to call attention to a word that bears a particularly strong meaning. This is, of course, different from our

---

[33] Another level 2 **stop** like **Shalshelet**, much more common, but perhaps not as strong.

[34] Wickes, *Two Treatises on the Accentuation of the Old Testament.*

[35] Jacobson, *Chanting the Hebrew Bible*, p. 105.

understanding: that the *Shalshelet* is brought on by the position of the word in the sentence and its syntactic function in relation to the words that follow. From the syntactic point of view, had a different verb been in the same position in the sentence, it would have been punctuated with the same *ta'am*.

As Amnon Shiloach writes in *Jewish Musical Traditions*, "In actual fact the biblical chant is not determined by musical standards, but is clarified from and subordinate to the punctuational values already determined by the accents."[36] The Grammarian has not been without influence.

The Grammarian's voice echoes in the Singer's ear, or at least in the ear of real live Torah readers, and it seems to undermine their confidence in what they hear. It may be the authority and logic in the voice of the Grammarian, or diffidence on the part of the Torah readers and their listeners, or simple reluctance to trust their instincts and what they hear in the chant. *Ba'alei keri'ah* often keep their insights to themselves. Here are a few examples:

- EXAMPLE 1: Genesis, Chapter 38, tells the story of Judah and Tamar. Tamar's businesslike seduction of Judah is described in a three-verse passage. There is a point/counterpoint quality in its trop, which enhances the drama of the text. Cantor Henry Rosenblum, dean of the cantorial school at the Jewish Theological Seminary of America, pointed out this feature to me. He had not mentioned this literary/musical insight before, and disclaimed: "I notice things like that but do not know what to make of them."

- EXAMPLE 2: A friend, Shu Kahn, e-mailed me, "I have this idea about the notes [*te'amim*] that I believe you disagree with. I see many of the notes as telling us something about the text." After describing a very interesting take on the story of the banishment of Ishmael and Hagar (Gen 18) in the light of the

---

[36] Shiloach, *Jewish Musical Traditions,* p. 103.

te'amim, she ended her communication with the question: "Am I crazy?"

- EXAMPLE 3: Cynthia Weber, when told of my project, shared a meaning that came to her when chanting a portion from the Prophets for the first time after converting to Judaism. Zechariah 3:5 reads: "Then I gave the order, 'Let a pure crown be placed on his head.' And they placed the pure crown on his head and clothed him in garments, as the angel of the Lord stood by." Cynthia noted the simplicity of the command contrasted with the richness of the actual event. This impression is present in the words themselves of course, but is more obvious in the chant, which called it to her attention. She went on to make an analogy to the transformation of her life in coming to Judaism, that the reality proved richer than she had anticipated. Cynthia has a musically sensitive ear. The device of elaboration in repetition is pervasive in Torah text and chant. Cynthia had not shared this valid insight with others.

I am not taking sides in the Grammarian-Singer debate. Those two need a marriage counselor and not a divorce judge. On the other hand, it is not a fair fight. The Grammarian has scholarship, logic, and footnotes. The Singer brings personal interpretation and feeling. So my first goal will be to level the playing field a little. At least with respect to **Shalshelet**, the Singer's point that it comes to dramatize the text is entirely correct, and this can be proven. It's not that the grammarians are wrong about the rules governing the behavior of **Shalshelet**; they have forgotten the nature of their enterprise — to uncover the logical rules of a musical system. A more holistic approach to trop is indicated. Here are four propositions:

- *Te'amei Hamikra* (the system of Cantillation — tunes, names of the *te'amim*, and eventually notation) serve primarily as a chant indicator, like musical notes today. The musical/chant function of *Te'amei Hamikra* precedes and is the basis for its grammatical function.

- There were clear traditions of chanting Scripture long before the development of written notation. The notation was not a later imposition on the text; rather, the chant is inherent in the text. The Torah was born in chant. Present chant traditions evolved from older ones and are the legitimate heirs of the ancient chant tradition.

- The reading of grammar into the *te'amim* is legitimate, but it is after-the-fact, analysis. What we are doing when we subdivide the *te'amim* into **connectors** and **stops** is to uncover the syntactical logic of biblical chant, the grammatical interpretation imposed on the verse by the rhythm and melody of the chant. In other words, biblical chant had a grammatical logic. The grammar of biblical chant is well explained in many texts.

- It is worth looking at how the music of the *te'amim* colors the experience of Torah, with respect to both rhythm/pace/emphasis and also melody, provided one tempers *ahavah* with *yir'ah* and **is careful to stay close to text**. This approach can be a valid and rich source of meaning.

Let us return to **Shalshelet.** If there were only three instances of **Shalshelet** in the Torah, the question, "Is it grammar or song?" could be considered debatable. But there is a fourth **Shalshelet**, and there the evidence is clear: **Shalshelet** Four has a dramatic, interpretive function. Ironically, this **Shalshelet** has been somewhat neglected. Indeed, it seems to come in what Wickes termed an "unimportant" location, in a verse that at first glance might seem not worth marking with special trop. Some have even stated that this appears to be an exception to the notion that **Shalshelet** comes to highlight a passage, as Schorsch noted in the Genesis passages. The next Chapter will take a closer look at the fourth **Shalshelet**.

Leviticus is usually put into a kind of glass cabinet: it can be looked at, respected, and wondered at, but the real heart of the religion is presumed to be found in other parts of the Bible, especially Genesis, Exodus, and Deuteronomy, and the writing of the psalmists and prophets. This tradition does Leviticus wrong.

Mary Douglas, *Leviticus as Literature*

Chapter 6
"And he slaughtered"
The Fourth Shalshelet:
Chant and Interpretation

DURING THE ANNUAL READING OF the Torah cycle, after the stories of Genesis and Exodus, and the stand at Sinai, we come to four months of readings, from Exodus 25 through Numbers 10, centering on the Tabernacle in the Wilderness and its sacrificial rite. If one does not read and listen carefully, these readings could easily seem boring and uninvolving, with very little redeeming material for the modern reader. Exodus 25-40 is mainly concerned with the building of the Tabernacle in the Wilderness. Leviticus deals with laws of sacrifices, purity, and the priesthood. The first two portions of Numbers are occupied with the encampment about the Tabernacle, and preparation for its journeys. The neglect of this part of the Torah has contributed to a lack of awareness of **Shalshelet** Four in Leviticus 8. In telling of a sacrificial service, it is harder to find the kind of emotional tension we see so readily in the Genesis stories. In terms of emotion, as Neil Gillman observes, "the fourth [**Shalshelet**], the one dealing with Moses' ordination of the *kohanim* [priests], is more of a stretch."[37] It would appear at first glance, that Wickes claim is correct. Perhaps **Shalshelet** Four occurs in a "mostly unimportant" text. Let's take a closer look.

Dedicating the Tabernacle

The readings about the Tabernacle and its sacrifices begin not in Leviticus, but in the last five *Parshiyot* — weekly readings — of Exodus. In *Teruma* and *Tetsaveh* (Exodus 25-30:10), Moses is given instruction on how to build the Tabernacle. After the episode of the golden calf (*Parashat Ki Tisa,* Exodus 30:11-34), Israel builds the Tabernacle (*Vayakhel -Pekudei,* Exodus 35-40). Virtually all the instructions to Moses in Chapters 25-30 are recapitulated in the recitation of the actual building in Chapters 35-40: all, that is, save one set of commands. An astute listener would notice that the inauguration of the Tabernacle was not fully accomplished by the end of Exodus. In Chapter 29, Moses is taught the ceremony for dedicating the Tabernacle and the priests. This ceremony is to precede the start of the sacrificial rite itself. The instructions on the dedication of the Tabernacle will not be enacted in Exodus, but in Leviticus.

As Leviticus opens, Moses is told to instruct the people on how to conduct the sacrificial rite. A permanent Temple in Jerusalem will ultimately replace the Tabernacle, but the sacrificial service described in Leviticus 1-7 will be the basis for Israel's worship of God for the next fifteen hundred years. The performance of the dedication ritual commanded in Exodus 29 will be told in Leviticus 8-10.

I will call these three chapters, in the heart of the Tabernacle material, "The Dedication Story." They form the only narrative unit of Leviticus,[38]

---

[37] Neil Gillman, Devar Torah, Long Island Jewish Press

[38] An apparent exception is the very brief account of the fate of the Israelite who curses God, Lev 23: 10-23. But this is not a "story" in the very rich biblical tradition. The violator is not named, and no motive discussed. It is a simple anecdote to serve as an example of case law, and is without emotional content.

and constitute a story in the full literary sense. "The Dedication Story" has a beginning, development, climax, and ending. It has vivid characters and emotional tension. Like all the Bible's great stories, it touches on critical spiritual and moral issues with sensitivity and complex insights. Here is a brief summary leading up to its climactic moment:

Leviticus 8 concludes *Parashat Tsav*, the second *parashah* of Leviticus. Moses assembles the people. He tells them that what they are about to witness is at the command of God. Moses' dressing of Aaron in his sacramental garments is described article by article. Moses anoints the Tabernacle and its contents with oil, and dresses the sons of Aaron in less elaborate garb. The following is an excerpt of what follows, from the narrative of Moses' sacrificial acts to consecrate the priests (Lev 8:14-29):

> And he led forward the bull of the *Hatat*; and Aaron and his sons laid their hands on the head of the bull of the *Hatat. And-he-slaughtered,* and Moses took the blood and put it on the horns of the altar around with his finger, and he purified the altar; and the blood he poured at the base of the altar, and consecrated it to atone it....

> Then he brought forth the ram of the *Olah*, and Aaron and his sons laid their hands on the head of the ram. *And-he-slaughtered;* and Moses dashed the blood on the altar around....

> Then he brought forward the second ram, the ram of *Miluim*; and Aaron and his sons laid their hands on the head of the ram. *AND-HE-SLAUGHTERED* [Shalshelet]?! and Moses took of the blood, and put it on Aaron's right ear, and on his right thumb, and on his right great toe. And he brought forward Aaron's sons, and Moses put of the blood on] their right ear, and on their right thumb, and on their right great toe; and Moses dashed the blood on the altar around...[39]

---

[39] Translation is adapted from JPS. The *Hatat, Olah,* and *Miluim* were three different kinds of sacrificial offerings. The *Hatat* was a purification offering, brought to atone for sins. The *Olah* or "burnt offering" is the main type of offering that would mark daily worship and festivals. The *Milu'im,* or ordination offering, was a special

After Moses' labors, Aaron and his sons are sequestered for seven days.

The details of processing the flesh of the animals were left out of the above translations, not because they were too gory, but because any English translation sounds bloody and crude. The Hebrew does not. The British anthropologist Mary Douglas has this to say about the sounds of Leviticus:

> Metrical form gives a structure to the work. It enhances the mood by making a match between the words of a song and the melody, or like the match between the words of the song, the rhythms of the music, and the bodily movements of the dance. The joy of a verbal rhyme is more than the match it makes with words, they have additional work to perform apart from what they do in the syntax: the words are there to ring consonances and make rhymed line endings that call attention to each other and give warning when the ending is near.... There is pleasure in seeing complex meanings separated, spread out, twisted. Folded over, and presented again, more shining and beautiful than ever.[40]

I concur with Douglas' sense of the sound-beauty of this part of the Torah, and tried to give a sense of Leviticus' effective use of repetition and rhythm in the above translation. The third repetition of the word *Vayish'chat* [*"AND-HE-SLAUGHTERED"*] is sung to the trop **Shalshelet**.

After Moses' consecration of the priest, *Parashat Tsav* comes to an end with the momentous and somewhat reassuring "And Aaron and his sons did *all the things* [emphasis in trop] God had commanded at the hand of Moses." We have to wait a week for *Parashat Shemini*, to read the continuation of our story, Leviticus 9: "And it was on the eighth day, Moses called Aaron and his sons...." As with many of our longer stories, the tradition chose to break the *parashah* at a climactic moment. Unlike the stories of Joseph and the Exodus, this break does not come at a spot of great tension. Everything has been going like clockwork. As the

---

offering for this particular occasion — the consecration of the priestly family for then and future generations.

[40] Douglas, *Leviticus as Literature,* p. 48.

eighth day begins, Aaron takes command of the sacrificial rite. His work culminates with wonder (Lev 9:24):

> And fire went forth from before the Lord, and consumed on the altar the *Olah* and the fat; and all the people saw and shouted joyously, and they fell on their faces.

It is a moment of great celebration.

Then tragedy strikes. In two terse verses we are told:

> And Aaron's sons Nadav and Avihu each took his fire-pan, and they put fire in them, and put incense on top of that, and they offered up before God a strange fire [*eish zara*], which He had not commanded them. And a fire went out from before God and consumed them; and they died before God.

Such are the perils of proximity to the sacred. At Moses' instruction, Aaron and his two remaining sons display no signs of grief or mourning. The bodies of the dead are removed. The service is brought to a close.

Whatever our conclusion about **Shalshelet**, Wickes' epithet "mostly unimportant" does not describe Moses' three sacrifices in *Parashat Tsav*. This is an extraordinary spot in an extraordinary narrative, calling for a heightened dramatization of the verse. Moses is about to cross a threshold. With his third sacrifice, Moses' work as Israel's intermediary is complete, and Aaron is fully capacitated as the High Priest. Israel will observe the sacrificial form of worship until the destruction of the Temple at the hands of the Romans some fifteen hundred years later. The intensity of the moment, the ardor of the people, and the dangerous proximity to the sacred are all highlighted in this story.

This is what Neil Gillman said was suggested to him by the *ta'am* **Shalshelet** in Leviticus 8, based on his interpretation of the three **Shalshelet**s of Genesis:

> ...since a *Shalshelet* always indicates ambivalence, we should assume that at this moment, the final step in the ordination of the

kohanim [priests], Moses too felt a certain kind of ambivalence. Was he reluctant to go through with the act because it now meant that he was now relinquishing the priesthood to his brother? That he was abandoning the central cultic role that he had enjoyed until now for that of a prophet alone? If so, that is a startling piece of *Midrash*.[41]

Let us leave for the moment the question of whether Rabbi Gillman is "correct" about what Moses may have been feeling at the time of the sacrifice. One thing is very clear, this particular word, performed to the tune **Shalshelet** in an Ashkenazi synagogue in the twenty-first century, will wake the sleepers, and call for interpretation: "What was that all about?" Rabbi Gillman responded to an obvious effect inherent in the performance of the passage. The first question, going back to our Singer-Grammarian debate, is whether that was an intentional effect as Gillman and Schorsch suggest? Or is it fortuitous and incidental, forced by the syntax of the verse, as Wickes and Jacobson would have it?

The evidence: 1) crescendo to Shalshelet

The phrase *"And-he-slaughtered"* occurs three times in Lev 8:14-29. It was hyphenated to give a better feel for the Hebrew, which is the single word *"Vayish'chat;"* such is the compactness of this language. How are the first two handled? What is their trop? I will need to introduce two other *te'amim*: **revi'a** and **etnachta**.

- The meaning of the word **revi'a** in Aramaic is "resting" or "settling down" (Jacobson, p.140). It is a level 3 **stop**. The Ashkenazi **revi'a** has a somewhat long, descending musical phrase, fitting the sense of coming to rest. It is not unusual for **revi'a** to come on the first word of a verse. It is my personal sense, as I noted in Chapter 4, that when **revi'a** opens a verse, it lends a slight emphasis to the first word, by hovering on it and extending it.

---

[41] Neil Gillman, Devar Torah, Long Island Jewish Press

- **Etnachta** also means "resting point." It is an even stronger level 1 **stop**, equal in rank to the period at the end of the verse. I suggest thinking of this *ta'am* as a semicolon that splits the verse into two. The great majority of verses in the Torah have an **etnachta**; there is never more than one in a verse. I call its sound a "tentative coda" in contrast to the definitive coda at the end of a verse. It is highly unusual to start a sentence with an **etnachta** on the first word (seventeen times in the Torah). Startling; it would be like having a semicolon after the first word in an English sentence.

I have tried to give a sense of what our passage would sound like when chanted in the translation above with a comma after "And-he-slaughtered" the first time (**revi'a**); the second time is in italics and followed by a semicolon (**etnachta**). The third (**Shalshelet**) is also in bold type and italicized. I would claim that this is faithful to the chant's "feel." Going from **revi'a** to **etnachta** to **Shalshelet** is a sort of natural crescendo, creating a sense of increasing tension and excitement. The buildup is palpable.[42] The fourth **Shalshelet** comes as a thunderclap.

Was the choice of **Shalshelet** forced by the syntax? Is Jacobson correct in saying that the choice of **Shalshelet** is forced by the grammar of the verse? Not at all. As Warren Wickes pointed out, the less dramatic **zakef gadol** would have done as well, and is the usual choice in a relatively short verse. **Shalshelet** in Lev 8:23 is an intentional touch to provide emphasis to the verse, and is not a simple grammatical choice.

But there is another even more important argument for this **Shalshelet**. All of the above reasoning tacitly assumes that we are given a text of words, and then figure out how to chant it, what trop to assign. The presumption is that the Masoretes, or perhaps an earlier source they relied on, "introduced" this trop to emphasize the verse. There is another possibility. Perhaps the librettist and composer are one; the writer of

---

[42] I am not the first to call attention to the progression of **revi'a**, **etnachta**, **Shalshelet** in this passage. See Weinberg, quoted in Goren, *Te'amei Hamikra Kefarshanut*, p. 76.

the text thought and wrote in Chant. In this case, we should find text and trop coordinated to provide the buildup of tension and significance noted above. And that is clearly the case here.

The evidence: 2) the argument from the text — unity of composition

I was aware from reading the text repeatedly in trop that there was something bothering me about the language of the passage, but had trouble putting my finger on it. At some point it struck me: the word "*Vayish'chat* — '*And-he-slaughtered*'" is awkward. And he slaughtered — *what*? "To slaughter" is a transitive verb in English or Hebrew. Throughout the Tanakh this verb generally takes a direct object. Apparently JPS and other translators also thought the language awkward, and intentionally mistranslated the verse by making the verb passive: "and it [the ox/ram] was slaughtered." They did not need to do so in this case. The correct translation sounds ungainly, but conveys an accurate sense of the strangeness of the Hebrew verse.

How unusual is it? The verb "to slaughter" occurs 43 times in Scripture. Except for these three occurrences in Lev 8 and one other readily explained instance,[43] "to slaughter" *always* has a direct object. The choice of language alone — leaving out the direct object of a transitive verb — would have made the verses interesting. Moreover, had the more usual language "And he slaughtered the [second] ram" opened verse 23, there could not have been a **Shalshelet**. A striking and unusual word choice was needed to enable the extreme emphasis of this verse in song.

The Grammarian might answer: "But perhaps, despite all the odds, this is just a series of coincidences. The wordcrafters might have felt that two mentions of the animal in the immediately preceding verse would serve to tell what was slaughtered. Perhaps they left it out of those three verses

---

[43] Leviticus 17:3: "Any man from the house of Israel who *will-slaughter* an ox, or a sheep, or a goat in the camp, or who *will-slaughter* outside the camp…" Here the Torah makes use of ellipsis within a verse, given the biblical convention of parallelism. Had this not been done, the verse would have had to use the more awkward *sounding* "or who *will-slaughter* an ox, or a sheep, or a goat outside the camp" a second time in the verse. The direct object is assumed from the first part of the verse.

out of considerations of rhythm and elegance of language. Perhaps they preferred **Shalshelet** to **Zakef** to simply give verse 23 a stronger pause after the word *"And he slaughtered."*

The Torah itself can answer this last suggestion of the grammarian, for it tells this story twice. Like the doubled description of the building of the Tabernacle, told first as a series of instructions, and then repeated nearly word for word in the tale of the construction, the dedication of the Tabernacle is also doubled. Moses is instructed on how to perform the ceremony in Exodus 29. Leviticus 8 is nearly identical to the Exodus passage, except for the change in verb "tense" from future/imperative (*"and-you-shall-slaughter"* or just *"slaughter"* [JPS]) to the "past tense" we find in our passage. But when Moses receives his instructions in Exodus, the Tabernacle is not yet built. Its construction is the first priority. The dedication ceremony must have seemed far off. There is no tension or drama in the planning. Absent as well are all the highlighting effects in Leviticus. Compare Ex 29:19-20 to the parallel Lev 8:22-23, which contains **Shalshelet** Four:

> Then you will take **the second ram**, and Aaron and his sons will lay their hands on the head of the ram. *And-you-will-slaughter* the **ram**, and take of its blood and you will put it on Aaron's right ear and on his sons' right ear, and on their right thumb, and on their right great toe; and you shall dash the blood on the altar around.

The syntax is standard — the direct object appears explicitly: *"And-you-will-slaughter **the ram**."* The object of "slaughter" is also made explicit also in verses 11 and 16.

This is a second piece of evidence that the Torah was accentuating and highlighting the moment of the Ordination sacrifice, and that in Leviticus text and chant are composed together. We proclaim in both word and song what we know from looking at Leviticus as a whole: "This is a one-time event, a special moment! Sit up and take notice!" The psychological insight of the Torah is often striking, and here is an example that is generally missed in a casual reading. Hearing about and planning an event feel different than actually accomplishing the act.

Moses in Exodus, learning about constructing the Tabernacle, might not have felt anxiety at the thought of performing the final ceremony. How different when it comes time to carry out the instructions! In addition to Rabbi Gillman's thoughtful questions about Moses' hesitation, I would wonder if Moses might have been fearful about turning over the priestly duties to his brother. Could he have had a premonition of the tragedy that was to come? Would he have sensed that sooner or later a member of his family would test the limit and come to harm? There is not one definite answer to these questions, but they hover in the air. In the midst of a part of the Torah that is occupied entirely with ritual acts, the *ba'al keri'ah* will call the listener to attend to the human side of this drama. Imagine one's reaction, seeing the confident leader Moses in an apparently rattled state! What does it mean that his hand shakes as he approaches the last sacrifice? Much as in real life, one is left to wonder about the thoughts, motives, and emotions of leaders and public figures. But there should be no doubt about the intensity of the moment.

The evidence: 3) Text in the light of trop

The final piece of evidence of the value of listening to the Torah through the medium of chant is the apparent validity of the approach. Trop, through musical interpretation, adds layers of complexity to text. These layers will be developed more fully in the rest of this book. I hope to convince the reader that this expanded view of the Dedication Story in Leviticus 8-10 is a plausible reading of the text, and that it presents a meaningful contribution to an ongoing 3000 year discussion of how calamity can occur in a world presided over by a just and loving God.

Trop, namely the fourth **Shalshelet**, suggested a "startling" reading of Leviticus 8, a description of the carrying out of the commandments of Exodus 29, much of it word for word repetition. It is straightforward to read these passages as mechanical descriptions of ritual acts, lacking aspects of behavior that make human action interesting. The predominant artistic device for calling attention to the emotional intensity and dramatic import of the moment is musical. Rabbi Gillman's interpretation based on what he heard in a public recitation serves as a demonstration of the way chant can call attention to an untapped potential meaning in what appeared to be a dry text. Which is the more plausible reading — full blown story or ritual account? Is the internal conflict in Moses yet another example of fanciful *Midrash*? Is trop opening a doorway into the world of Scripture or merely leading us into a wondrous garden of fanciful musings just outside?

In the next two chapters, we will examine the rest of the story, Leviticus 9 and 10. Taken as a whole, "The Dedication Story" has the coherence of a literary piece:

- A beginning — Lev 8, the consecration of Aaron and his sons

- A middle section (Lev 9-10:7)

    — Aaron takes over on the eighth day, his ritual acts leading up to:
    - Climax — the leaders' blessing and the miraculous acceptance of the people's sacrifice
    - Sudden reversal and tragedy — the death of Aaron's eldest two sons
- Denouement — resolution

It is hard to imagine that this tight structure is coincidental or fanciful. In the words of the storyteller and writer Wendy Besmann: "In fact, this story construction seems to be an innate feature of storytelling, transcending the bounds of time and culture. We naturally act out a story in this fashion — build up, climax, and follow-up. Why would chant not reflect this compelling human inclination?"

Stories, as opposed to myths and legends, require fully rounded characters with complex psychology. The Tanakh's stories are notable for their vividness and complex character development. Abraham, Joseph, and David spring to life from its pages. Moses and Aaron have always been harder to read. The Torah gives only limited anecdotes involving Aaron and his actions. Over the centuries Moses has become progressively larger than life, so that we lose his human dimensions. **Shalshelet,** with its sound and its associations with emotional turmoil, is a wake-up call: "Feel the intensity of the moment. Imagine what is going through Moses' mind as he performs this rite. Wonder what it must mean that he betrays emotional conflict at this moment." These directions lead us to see legitimate emphases in the text that we otherwise might miss. Moses dominates the Torah as no other character, and yet there is a paucity of personal anecdotes about his life and adventures. We glimpse his public acts, with few intimate, private moments. More than any other of the Bible's leading personalities he has a tendency to stay out of reach, a gigantic, solitary leader. After his stay atop the mountain, his face is so radiant that one must look away. Chant restores perspective. He is human after all, with recognizable emotions.

Understanding characters in stories, and more particularly in theater, requires enlisting and aiding the imagination of the audience. Recall Franz Rosenzweig's metaphor — Torah as script; and its public chanting, *keri'ah*, as performance. And let us also return to the example of Shakespeare. Today, four centuries after his plays were written, relatively definitive texts of the plays exist. But we also have records of how directors have played scenes over the ages. A good dramaturge will research these; so that a production seen today partakes of the vision of its present director, but is also informed by performances of the past. I still remember my first viewing of a Shakespeare play: *Julius Caesar* at Old Vic's Theater in London, in the summer of 1962. My brother and I had been fond of reciting the line, "Friends, Romans, countrymen, lend me your ears; I come to bury Caesar, not to praise him," and would do so in a high, oratorical tone. I was surprised at the performance. Marc Antony had to interrupt a muttering angry crowd with these words, and did so as a rushed, urgent cry, designed to get their attention if only for a moment. Ever since, I have been more aware of the touches that the director puts in each performance that animate what might otherwise be a dry, archaic text.

When we see Shakespeare today, there is an overlay of text, past interpretation, the vision of the director and dramaturge of this performance, and what we ourselves witness and read into it. And the plays remain alive, still capable of holding up a mirror to the real world. Torah too is enhanced and brought to life by a good *keri'ah*. As the reader sings the story of Moses' last ritual performances, there is opportunity for dramatic expression. The words "And-he-slaughtered" are read with a building tension. At the third and final sacrifice, the ram of Ordination, a wavering long melody wakes its listeners. To those who remember the Genesis readings, it will plainly suggest that the great spiritual leader is in turmoil. On the verge of world-changing events, it may be difficult for a thoughtful person to act. Genesis' **Shalshelet** spoke to three types of internal conflict. Lot's hesitation, the uncertainty of Abraham's servant, and Joseph's temptation are all rolled into the moment that Moses confronts at the dedication of the *Mishkan*. Rabbi Gillman has commented on how his hearing of Torah affected his understanding of a passage: "The full effect of the **Shalshelet** is one further reminder, if one is needed, of the power of the weekly Torah reading, and of our need to insure that the Torah be read with precision and artistry. Only then will its full power be felt."[44]

---

[44] Neil Gillman, Devar Torah, Long Island Jewish Press

And I will meet there with the Children of Israel, and it [the *Mishkan*] will be made holy through my glory.

Exodus 29: 43

And Moses said to Aaron, "That is what God spoke, saying, 'I shall be made holy through those who are close to me, and I shall be glorified in front of all the people.'"

Leviticus 10: 3

Holy, holy, holy is the Lord of Hosts; the fullness of the world is his glory.

Isaiah 6: 3

Blessed is the glory of the Lord from its place.

Ezekiel 3: 12

Chapter 7
"On the eighth day..."
The Strangest Trop in Torah

SHALSHELET IS THE MOST FAMILIAR of the "rare accents" of the *Te'amei Hamikra*, but it is not the only one. The story of the dedication of the Tabernacle in Leviticus 8-10 is marked by three other instances of rare trop, more than any other passage in the Torah. As was the case with **Shalshelet**, these additional instances will suggest a more interesting interpretation of the text than is usually imagined, revealing a literary gem with fully developed characters and intense emotions. The tale that emerges connects with other parts of Torah, with deep insights about core ideas of the Jewish religion. Chant

95

prods us to ask, what is so unusual about this story that it calls for such unusual music? Let's pick up the story where we left off.

On the eighth day of dedication, the *Mishkan* is fully erected. Trop drew attention to the intensity of Moses' acts in the sacrificial service of the previous seven days. Aaron's first ceremonial acts on Day Eight are described in Leviticus, Chapter 9. All goes well. Aaron's sacrifices are received in a spectacular fashion, to the wonder of the people. Then tragedy strikes. The transgression of Aaron's sons Nadav and Avihu, their immediate incineration, and Moses' response to the situation are compactly narrated in Lev 10:1-7. Those seven verses have three separate instances of rare trop combinations, the highest density anywhere in the Torah. Here is the text (Lev 9:24-10:7); I have highlighted the three unusual trop moments:

> And fire came forth from before the Lord, and consumed on the altar the *Olah* and the fats; and all the people saw and shouted in joy, and fell on their faces. And Aaron's sons Nadav and Avihu, each took his fire-pan, and they put fire in them, and put incense on top of that; and they offered up before God a strange fire [*eish zara*], which he had *not* commanded them. And a fire went out from before God, and consumed them; and they died before God. And Moses said to Aaron, "That is what God spoke saying, 'I shall be made holy through those who are close to me[45], and I shall be glorified in front of all the people;'" and Aaron became silent.

> And Moses called, to Mishael and to Eltzaphan, sons of Uziel, Aaron's uncle; and he said to them, "*Draw close,* carry your brothers from in front of the Holy, to the outside of the camp." And they came close, and carried them in their tunics, to the outside of the camp; as Moses had spoken.

> And Moses said to Aaron, and to Elazar and Ithamar his sons, "*Do not let loose the hair of your heads, and do not tear your clothes, and you will not die,* and He'll be angry at the entire congregation; and

---

[45] This long phrase "I shall...close to me" is just two words in Hebrew, elliptical and obscure: "*bikrovai ekadesh.*"

your brothers, all the house of Israel, will weep for the burning, which God has burned. And from the doorway of the Tent of Meeting, you shall not go out, lest you die, for God's anointing oil is upon you;" and they did according to Moses' word.

The emphasized phrases are all instances of extraordinarily rare trop or trop combinations. We may again be reminded of Wickes' contention that rare trop occurs in "mostly unimportant" passages. The story of the deaths of Aaron's sons is brief and relatively unfamiliar. It has not dominated the popular imagination, as have the stories of Genesis or the stand at the Red Sea, for example. Prior to listening carefully to this passage, and the features that are jarring when read aloud, I had not noticed the intense human drama.

It is easy to miss. The eight verses above do not begin a new paragraph in the Torah, but are the conclusion to the narration of the events of the eighth day of dedication of the *Mishkan*. They are abrupt and spare in detail. The usual reading sees Aaron as understandably upset. Moses is imperious and cool, perhaps unfeeling, when he commands that the ceremony should continue. Aaron shows no sign of mourning. The only indication of Aaron's feelings is the observation: "and Aaron became silent," in which some commentators (see Rashbam for example) have seen the implication that he had been weeping. I have not found a commentary that considers what Moses' state of mind would have been. A closer look at the passage will change the impression that the protagonists' feelings are given short shrift. As with **Shalshelet** earlier in this story, trop calls attention to a moment that is emotionally intense and fraught with meaning.

It is terrible to lose a child. As I start to write this Chapter, I have just returned from a three month Sabbatical and resumed my duties as a family physician. Reminders of human frailty are unbearably close. Yesterday, I attended the funeral of a dear friend and patient who died of cancer. His daughter reflected that my patient began to go downhill when her brother, his youngest son, killed himself a year previously. A country doctor is never far from such stories. Returning from my

Sabbatical in New York to my practice in East Tennessee I am again in contact with the maelstrom of human life. On the day I wrote this Chapter, I encountered a favorite patient, an older gentleman who had lost over fifty pounds after no more than the suggestion that he become more active and drink less soda. His visits are always full of fun — his chosen exercise was square dancing with his wife. I had last seen him about seven months ago. Today when I asked how his life had been going, his face became contorted with the effort not to cry: "Terrible. My daughter was killed in a car accident seven months ago. Nothing's still not right."

So how can we tell the story of Nadav and Avihu as an object lesson to adhere to scrupulous standards in following God's commands or to avoid drunkenness when carrying out priestly duties? How can we imagine an imperious and cool Moses telling his brother to show no sign of mourning and to carry on? How can we envision an Aaron so "saintly" as to earn God's blessing and forgiveness by being quiet at a time like this? How can the Torah tell this story as if the humanity of the characters is insignificant? When we tell this story at all — and it is not one of the stories we tend to dwell on — this is largely how we tell it. And when we listen to it closely, we are bothered by it. Many commentators have noted that it is unclear precisely what the two brothers did that merited such severe retribution, if retribution it was. The trop on this passage can lead us to hear this passage with different ears. It will not become easier. But it is richer and more sensitive than has been imagined. Turbulent emotions become plain in the very spare text. The music of the chant will call attention to them.

There are three very rare trop combinations in this passage. **Singularity One**: in verse 1, the *ta'am* on the word "not" is **mercha kefula** (double **mercha**), a *ta'am* which occurs only five times in the Torah and fourteen in all of the "twenty-one books." **Singularity Two**: in verse 4, on the word "draw-near" there are two **stop** trop on one word: **telisha gedola** and **gershayim**. This combination occurs only one other time in the Torah. **Singularity Three**: verse six, which has a decidedly herky-jerky feel both in text and trop, has the awkward trop sequence **mercha-**

legarmeh-mahpach-pashta. This sequence occurs only one other place in Torah,[46] a place with a very clear connection to this passage in language, theme, and music.

What does the music tell us? As with **Shalshelet** we must ask the very important questions: What is permitted in looking at an ancient text, which has been worked over in so many ways? When is an interpretation "fanciful," reflecting more one's own perspectives than Torah's intention? I will make the case that Torah was sensitive to the turbulent emotions of Moses and Aaron, and depicted them with clear and vivid composition in chant, despite the limitations of its narrative conventions. I will also hold this interpretation up to the standard that I have suggested for examining musical insights. Is literary composition present in the text, or simply the "fanciful *Midrash*" of a twentieth century rural doc who has weathered losses with many of his families?

This Chapter will first explore the three rare chant themes in the passage, and their connections. Each of these three "works" in a slightly different way. We will then step back, and look at how these connections illuminate the passage as a whole, suggesting a new reading. We will see how this reading resonates with older voices. And we will have cause for reflection on the process of interpretation and how chant illuminates text.

Singularity One: mercha kefula – ambiguity

In 1966, David Weisberg wrote an article spread out over three issues of the *Jewish Quarterly Review* on "The Rare Accents of the Twenty-One Books." He dealt with **Shalshelet**, another rare trop **karne fara**, and with the third of the rare *te'amim*, **mercha kefula**. This *ta'am* occurs on the word "not" in the first verse of our passage, Lev 10:1. **Mercha kefula**

---

[46] Its only other occurrence in the rest of Scripture is Ruth 1:2. Unlike Shalshelet and Singularities One and Two, which would be noted by an untrained listener, this trop sequence does not have a dramatic sound. The grammarians (See Wickes for example) have been aware of how unusual it is and singled it out for comment. This music occurs in the naming of two ill-fated brothers, one the husband of Ruth. The brothers are also destined to die, in a fateful story of tragedy turning to triumph. Coincidence?

occurs only five times in Torah. There are another nine instances in the rest of the Tanakh.[47] Weisberg comments: "Surprisingly, almost every source has neglected the problem of whether there is any discernible reason for the introduction of the ... special accents at various points in the Masoretic text!" He concludes, "These accents ... are devices introduced by the Masoretes to connect certain Biblical words with homiletic interpretations." In the case of **mercha kefula** (literal meaning: double **mercha**), he has the sense that the trop refers to a tale from *Midrash* connected with the word in question. He analyzes seven of the fourteen occurrences in the Tanakh, and uncovers *Midrashim* for each.

Weisberg's article can be used as a take-off point. His list of all the occurrences of the rare *te'amim* is useful. I differ with Weisberg in one respect. It is unlikely that the Masoretes were using trop as a means of flagging rabbinic legends. As discussed in Chapter 3, their mission was to faithfully transmit a received tradition of how Scripture is pronounced in public chant. The Masoretes were meticulous in their task. What little writings and notes they left are preoccupied with the intricacies of grammar and not with legends or elaborate interpretations.

Weisberg does not note that of the fourteen occurrences of the *ta'am* **mercha kefula**, eight of them are on the word "*la*" [hers], "*lo*" [his], or its homonym "*lo*" [no or not]. Two others occur immediately after the very similar word "*halo*" [is it not?]. The *Midrashim* Weisberg cites on these verses generally reflect ambiguity that could come from flipping these meanings ("hers" versus "not," for example). Could it be that the "**double mercha**" comes to highlight a word or phrase with a double meaning? If the Masoretes preserved an ancient chant tradition, they would have provided a clue as to how the Sages heard Torah recited. If there is rabbinic *Midrash* on these verses, that may be due to their hearing the *ba'alei keri'ah* of *their* time creating an unusual effect. Highlighting

---

[47] Gen 27:25, Ex 5:15, Lev 10:1, Num14:3 and 32:42, I Kings 10:3 and 20:29, Ezek 14:4, Habakuk 1: 3, Zechariah 3:2, Ezra 7:25, Nehemiah 3:38, II Chronicles 9:2 and 20:30.

an ambiguous word in the sacred text would have stimulated comments and thoughts in Mishnaic times, much like in ours.

What about **mercha kefula** in our passage in Leviticus? Ambiguity in this text was noticed long ago, without any explicit reference to the trop. It relates back to the hard question that lingers over this passage: was Nadav and Avihu's error so grievous as to merit death?

Nechama Leibowitz, the noted exegete of the last century, clarifies the double interpretations of the verse,[48] first commenting:

> Ostensibly, the reason for the punishment is evident:
>
> 10:1   **And offered strange fire before the Lord, which he commanded them not.**
>
> However, this verse harbors an ambiguity pointed out by Baal haTurim [classical commentator, fifteenth century Spain] who offers the following solution:
>
> > …This does not read A) He had not commanded them to bring strange fire; neither B) that He had not commanded them not to bring. Rather "which He commanded them not" means "which He commanded them: 'not!'"

In the view of the Baal haTurim, it was not just that the brothers had decided to add a ritual that they had not been commanded, but that they had been explicitly commanded not to do such an act. In his view this prohibition is contained in the admonition regarding the golden incense altar (Exodus 30:9): "You shall offer no strange incense [*ketoret zara*] on it." Leibowitz cites other commentators who justify this reading of the verse before finally noting that this is not the way most have read the verse: "the majority of the commentators deny that there was a negative or positive commandment concerning the offering." One even insists on the opposite reading:

---

[48] "The Sin of the Sons of Aaron," p. 118-127. *Further Studies in Vayikra.*

"which He did not command them": There is an implicit praise in the censure. They only performed what they were not commanded to do, but not that which they were commanded not to do.

Leibowitz pointedly asks, "Yet how can their severe punishment be explained?" If **mercha kefula** often highlights ambiguity, here it calls further attention to this perplexing question.[49]

Singularity Two: two trop on one word

When two trop occur on one word, it is usually a **stop** and its serving **connector**. Two places in Torah and five in Tanakh,[50] the *te'amim* **Geresh** and **Telisha Gedola** occur on the same word. One of these is in our passage, Lev 10:4 on the word "Draw near." It could be argued that this is accidental. Both of these *te'amim* are level 4 (the weakest) **stops**. They are pretty much interchangeable and have the same grammatical effect. Perhaps there were simply two traditions of how to chant the verse, and the Masoretes rather than taking sides, simply recorded both as valid choices to the reader. Our current tradition, perhaps reflecting a concern to make sure we include the correct *ta'am*, is to read them both, the **Geresh** before the **Telisha**. But is it likely that this unusual trop combination came about in so incidental a manner? What do the other occurrences tell us?

The first occurrence of this unusual trop combination, and the only other one in the Torah, is in a place of plausible emphasis. At the end of the highly repetitive "begats" at the end of *Parashat Bereishit*, the list pattern is broken as we are told of the birth of the first historically significant

---

[49] There is ambiguity in the sound of the reading, a disconnect between the meaning we might derive from the music and grammar of the trop. **Mercha kefula** is a longish musical phrase; listening to melody I might hear, "…that 'Not!' He commanded them." On the other hand, **mercha kefula** is a mere **connector** and should not be used to separate words; grammatically the Masoretic reading is "…that He did not command them." Listening to a meticulous *ba'al keri'ah*, a listener will hear both ideas simultaneously. It is left open to personal interpretation and subjective hearing whether Exodus 30:9 did or did not pertain to the actions of the young priests.

[50] Gen 5:29, Lev 10:4, II Kings 17:13, Ezek 48:6, Zephaniah 2:9.

figure since Adam — Noah (Genesis 5:29). Noah's father, Lemech, names him, saying, "*This-one* [**Geresh/Telisha**] *will comfort us from our toil and the pain of our hands, from the soil which God had cursed.*" Of course, Noah does not exactly turn out to give comfort to the rest of mankind. This too turns out to be a tale of destruction and punishment for sin. And (coincidence?), so do the three other occurrences in the "Prophets" division of Tanakh. Here they are:

The first occurrence of **Geresh/Telisha** in the prophetic books is in II Kings, 17. This passage deals with the exile of the Northern Kingdom of Israel by Assyria. The Tanakh is clear that the people are exiled because of their sins in straying from God's commands. They had set up places of worship "on every high hill and under every leafy tree." They had continued to stray, even though God had warned: "*Turn-back* [**Geresh/Telisha**] from your wicked ways…*"

The second occurrence of **Geresh/Telisha**, in Ezekiel 48:6, comes toward the end of the book. The prophet shares his vision of the final restoration of Israel, and the rebuilding of the Temple. Ezekiel prophesied in Babylon to the people recently exiled after the destruction of the First Temple in Jerusalem in 586 B.C.E. His writings include the well-known vision of the valley of dry bones. Bone joins bone, becomes flesh, and finally the breath of life is restored. This vivid metaphor provided hope for the exiles. The return of the exiles to their homeland when Persia conquered Babylon is traditionally seen as the fulfillment of this prophecy. The last part of the Book of Ezekiel contains the prophet's vision of the restoration of the Temple and its sacrificial service. In Chapter 48, after describing the land to be set aside for the Temple, Ezekiel turns to the portion of the land reserved for the priests. "*And-to-these* [**Geresh/Telisha**] shall be the sacred reserve of the priests…*" Which priests? "This consecrated area shall be for the priests of the line of Zadok, who kept my charge and did not go astray, as the Levites did when the people of Israel went astray." This is a reference to Chapter 44. There Ezekiel speaks to those priests who aided and abetted the people in their straying during the first Temple period, before the exile. Israel had committed the dual abominations of admitting the uncircumcised to the Temple grounds and worshipping idols. Many of the priests, with the exception of the Zadok clan, apparently helped the people in their pagan worship. The punishment of the erring priests was that they would be removed from the priesthood. Instead they would serve the descendants of Zadok in the demoted role of Levites.

The last occurrence of **Geresh/Telisha** is in the book of Zephaniah, one of the Twelve Minor Prophets. It is a short book of only three chapters. Zephaniah is occupied with a vision of restoration as well. Retribution will fall on the nations that have beleaguered Israel, and Israel will return to its land. Her renown and fame will be restored. Most of the text is devoted to prophecy of retribution, and the most vivid detail is reserved for Assyria and its great city Nineveh: "*Is-this* [**Geresh/Telisha**] the gay city that dwelt secure, that thought in her heart, 'I am, and there is none but me'?" Zephaniah's word "Is this" is reminiscent of Noah's "This one" in speaking of comfort [to Israel] and destruction [of its enemies] simultaneously. It also recalls the verse just mentioned in Kings 17. Assyria was responsible for the exile of the Northern Kingdom of Israel.

The common theme of destruction, punishment, and comfort permeates all of these texts. That seems more than just a coincidence, but I will leave the reader to speculate on whether or not this connection is real or fanciful. For me, in any case, it came after the fact. It's not as if, when I read the word "Draw near," I said, "Aha! This must be about comfort and destruction." The combination of these two *te'amim* is one that we have considered in Chapter 5 in Abraham's argument with God over the fate of Sodom and Gomorrah. Chant seemed to signal a change in Abraham's tone from challenging to hesitant, consistent with the change in the words. That too, of course, was a tale of punishment and destruction. In Leviticus, these same two trop in reversed order also strike a tremulous note musically. They raise the question, was Moses truly composed and businesslike as he worked to salvage the day? Like lines in a script, Moses' words in this passage are without dramatic direction. They can be read flatly, or in an imposing, commanding voice. But chant prolongs the word "draw near," and gives it an emotional quaver. Perhaps Moses was shaky and unsure of himself. In suggesting that an emotional reading is correct and not just a fanciful imposition on the text, I am not relying merely on psychological plausibility. There is a third "extraordinary trop moment" in the story, and text will support this view as well.

Singularity Three: the strangest of all

> And Moses said to Aaron, and to Elazar and Ithamar his sons, **"Do not let loose the hair of your heads, and do not tear your clothes, and you will not die,** and He'll be angry at the entire congregation; and your brothers, all the house of Israel, will weep for the burning, which God has burned.
>
> Leviticus 10:6

There is almost nothing right about this verse, and I first became aware of its awkwardness in preparing to read it in chant.[51] Now this is Leviticus. There is a mastery of word craft and chant that has always made Leviticus one of my favorite books to read, for the sheer elegance of its sound. This verse is lacking the usual smoothness. In the translation, I was careful not to rewrite the phrase "and He'll be angry at the entire congregation," which comes off as blurted out, an expression of fear about the fate of the entire flock. The awkwardness of this verse seems to have been missed by commentators and translators alike. Of many translations I sampled,[52] only Richard Friedman was daring enough to

---

[51] The trop goes awry from the start. From **Pazer** on "Aaron," to **Telisha** on "Elazar," to the **Pasek** between "Ithamar/his sons," the trop has trouble flowing. This fitful start further accentuates the jerkiness of the underlined part of the verse. *Ba'alei keri'ah* among the readers are invited to try this verse for themselves, and see how difficult it is to get it right, how "clumsy" it feels, in the words of Warren Rogers, a friend I had try the exercise.

[52] King James, JPS (1917 and 1962 versions), Art Scroll Stone Edition, Alter, and Everett Fox all depart from the Masoretic punctuation to render the verse more sensible and flowing. For example, JPS 1917 reads, "that ye die not, and that he be *not* [this word absent from the Hebrew] wroth with the entire congregation." Or Fox: "so that you do not die and he be furious with the entire congregation." JPS renders, "Do

render the verse into English that mimics the painful choppiness of the chanted Hebrew.

Is the awkwardness of this verse in trop and syntax accidental? Does it represent sloppy writing? Is it perhaps a corrupted verse, changed from a better lost version? Here again chant will help us. The verse contains a "forbidden" trop combination that occurs only one other place in Torah. It is striking enough for William Wickes, the nineteenth century Gentile accentuologist, to have noted its uniqueness. And its echo later in Leviticus is a clear reference to our text.

The trop sequence that bothered Wickes, on the phrase *"Do not let loose the hair of your heads and do not tear your clothes"* is "**mercha legarmeh, mahpach pashta.**" **Legarmeh** is typically followed by "**munach revi'a**" or "**munach zarka.**" The usual trop would work, if the phrase "and you shall not die" were deleted. The presence of this phrase mandates the longer sequence. The trop suggests that Moses is unsure of his speech, starting out to say one thing, and then changing directions midthought. I picture Moses starting out to caution Aaron and his remaining sons not to depart from the scheduled ritual, and not to ruin their elaborate dress. As he is uttering this, he is immediately aware of how inappropriate this might seem to the family, and quickly adds, "so that you don't die." Moses can't keep from blurting out his deepest fears "and He'll be angry at the entire congregation." In a final conciliatory note he recognizes that they can't be satisfied with going on as if nothing has happened. The rest of Israel will mourn the "burning that God has burned." He cannot bear to mention the deaths of his nephews explicitly.

This intricate reading of Leviticus 10:6 fits the trop in both its musical and grammatical functions. It is again appropriate to examine if this musico-rhythmic interpretation is a valid reading of the text. Am I reading too much into a single verse? Does the Torah truly contain

---

not dishevel your hair and do not rend your clothes, lest you die and anger strike the whole community." These are utterances that might have been said by a Moses who feels secure and in command, but the Moses featured here is in pain and not a little panic. His speech is urgent, rushed, and heedless of smooth expression.

this much intentional literary artistry? Is this third singularity simply the product of the grammatical needs of an awkward verse? Where is the only other use of this trop anyway? That ought to shed light on these questions. In fact, it leaves little room for doubt.

Leviticus 21 is occupied with conduct and physical requirements of priests, descendants of Aaron, who perform God's sacred service. They are not allowed to come in contact with the dead, except for their closest family members, such as parents, children, siblings, and wives. The High Priest must be even more scrupulous (verses 10-12):

> And the priest who is greatest of his brothers, **on whose head is poured the anointing oil, and who is appointed** to wear the clothes: *he shall not let loose the hair of his head, and shall not tear his clothes.* And he shall not come to any dead persons; for his father and mother he shall not become impure. And he shall not go out from the sanctuary, and shall not desecrate his God's sanctuary, for the crown of *God's anointing oil is on him*; I am the Lord.

The underlined phrase is the other occurrence of our Singularity Three trop combination, **"mercha-legarmeh-mahpach-pashta munach zakef."** The words in italics are echoes of Leviticus 10, this time with "normal" trop. The musical motif is identical. The literary theme is the same. The High Priest — anointed, inaugurated, dressed in special garments — is so sacred to God that he cannot come into contact with anything that would confer ritual impurity, even the bodies of his closest relatives. The High Priest is unique — separate from the rest of humanity. Trop reminds us of the inauguration of the first High Priest in "The Dedication Story." Music gives reason to reflect on the terrible price the High Priest pays for filling this office, the loneliness, the pain. It is a reminder of the demands of the office, and the consequences of deviation from its stringent requirements.

Coincidence? Hardly! This verse in Leviticus 21 does not require a "forbidden" trop sequence singularity to work grammatically. The singularity, in fact, comes on a different phrase, even though the original phrase *"he shall not let loose the hair of his head, and shall not tear his clothes*" from Leviticus 10 occurs in the verse. The verse contains word echoes of the earlier story. Such word echoes are a recognized feature of biblical narrative art. So, it would seem, are the musical echoes of the chant tradition.

Richard Friedman's translation of the story of Nadav and Avihu is particularly sensitive, and he too hears the emotionally charged description of the passage:

> Aaron's inaugural day of priestly sacrifice is thus to have been a glorious day of pomp and ceremony, miraculously sanctioned by the divine glory and fire; but then this extraordinary thing happens.... After seven chapters of laws of sacrifices, and two chapters describing the ordination rituals, the sudden account of this horrible event in the middle of the ceremonies comes as a shock.... The story of Nadav and Abihu is ...to be understood as a horror that occurs during the inauguration of the priesthood.

> Their pain is a reminder that the standard for leaders is *tougher* than others. According to the Torah, leaders do not get away with more because of their position. Priests, prophets, kings, rabbis, presidents: they suffer *harder* consequences.

Friedman is on target in describing this episode in the larger "Dedication Story" in terms such as "extraordinary," "horrible," "sudden," and "shocking." Trop goes beyond calling attention to a pivotal and intense moment. It transforms the mood of these verses, provides a peek into the emotional life of the characters, and hints at wider Scriptural connections of the story.

The question remains, why did Chant focus so many unusual devices on this story? Scriptural stories are more than good yarns meant to divert or amuse. The intricate plot devices and lively characterization are pathways to understanding ourselves, the universe, and the relationship of human and Divine. Trop revealed a tale buried in the heart of Torah. What is so important about this story? If trop is a doorway into the world of Scripture, where has it led us? We return to Nechama Leibowitz's original conundrum, still unanswered: "How can their severe punishment be explained?"

Righteous is God in all his ways; and lovingly kind in all his deeds.

Psalm 145

Blessed are you God, King of the universe, who fashions light and creates darkness, who makes peace and creates everything.

Opening blessing of the morning *Shema* service

Blessed are you God, King of the universe, the true judge.

Blessing, recited by a mourner on hearing of
the death of a close relative

Chapter 8
Justice and Mercy

IN THE LAST CHAPTERS, I HAVE discussed the ways in which chant changes the manner of hearing four different verses from a story at the heart of the Torah, Leviticus 8-10. Music has suggested that two moments in the dedication of the Tabernacle in the Wilderness — Moses' last sacrifice and the deaths of his two nephews — were emotionally charged and turbulent for both him and his brother Aaron. So what? If I were left with only a good yarn, I would not have felt such strong inner compulsion to talk about Torah reading and what chant does to word. Rather, I'm convinced that the question, "How can their severe punishment be explained?" is woven deeply into the fabric of this story. Theodicy is not new, and in one form or another has been one of the most significant questions that any religion must address.

Jewishly, we might phrase it: How can terrible suffering exist if the world is the creation of a just and loving God? Worse yet, how can tragedy be part of the Divine Plan? Here, this question is presented not as an abstract proposition, but in a powerful and personal narrative setting: at the height of Israel's celebration of freedom and intimate closeness to the Divine, this most nagging and persistent of questions intrudes itself. I'd like to demonstrate with a careful, trop-sensitive reading that these concerns are central in Torah's moral and theological narrative.

So I will retell the "Dedication Story" in the light of its intense trop, and in its wider setting in the Torah. I will use traditional texts and personal experience to discuss how the bereaved are comforted in the Jewish tradition. I will examine the significance of the Tabernacle in Israel's national saga. I will look at the polar qualities of Divine justice and compassion manifest in this tale. And I will conclude by reflecting on the value of uncovering the voice of Scripture as a chanted work, called out in public recitation.

Dedicating the Tabernacle—a reprise

Flashback to Exodus 19: it is the third day of Israel's stand before Sinai. The people are about to receive the Ten Commandments. Amidst thunder and lightning God speaks to Moses and tells him to — one more time — go down to the foot of the mountain and warn the people to stand back from the mountain. Even the priests are not to draw near, lest God "break out in them." Moses is baffled; he has *already* warned the people. Nevertheless, God repeats his warning: "Don't let the people come close." No harm will befall that day. God's presence is frightening to the people. After their first taste of revelation, they beseech Moses to serve as their intermediary — they are convinced they will die if they experience another such revelation. This is the first caution. Proximity to holiness carries great risk and God will not keep those who approach uninvited from coming to harm. It is like a warning not to touch a high power electrical cable. Righteous or wicked, the careless are doomed. As Richard Friedman reflects on the deaths of Nadav and Avihu, "The point is that the text does not deal with their motives because that is not the issue. In the realm of the ritual, they have failed to observe a boundary, and so their fate is settled. This is one of several biblical stories that indicate that on the highest levels of the ritual realm, intention does not matter."

This is correct, but does not entirely satisfy. What about justice and fairness? What about those who died, or those left behind? Friedman suggests that these are modern qualms and were not the preoccupation of the Torah. He reflects here the correct admonition of archeology and biblical scholarship, which cautions to avoid reading modern perspectives into ancient texts. The shortcoming of this perspective is that it does not always accord the ancients the respect they deserve for their remarkable insight into the human condition and their moral sophistication.

We are hardly the first generation to ask why bad things happen to good people. The sages noted that it was common to find "a righteous person who has it bad, and a wicked person who has it good."[53] This awareness and the spiritual angst which accompanies it surface repeatedly in Scripture. One example, discussed earlier, is the story of Abraham's argument with God from Genesis. God mulls over Israel's mission in the world "to do righteousness and justice." He hesitantly hints to Abraham that he may be on the verge of destroying Sodom and Gomorrah for their wickedness. Abraham responds with immediate outrage. How can God do this? "Will the judge of all the earth not do justice?" It takes an elaborate bargaining session for Abraham to reach a sense of peace with God's plan. Yet another example can be found in the *Haftarah* (additional prophetic reading) for *Parashat Shmeini* which contains "The Dedication Story." King David (II Samuel, 6) has decided to bring Moses' Ark of the Covenant to his new capital. His faithful servant Uzzah, in an impulse to protect the Ark of the Covenant on its journey to Jerusalem, reaches to steady it. He dies instantly. This seems so wrong that an angry David temporarily abandons the project. Israel has long insisted on trying to understand Divine acts, and not accepting them as matters of caprice or simple inevitability.

---

[53] Berakhot 7a.

Friedman makes a valid point about the peril of crossing a sacred boundary, but it is also plausible that the Leviticus writer would have been preoccupied with the heavy moral questions the story raises. How could a just and merciful God allow such a terrible tragedy to mar the dedication of his house? The "answer" that Leviticus offers is intricate and involves theological concepts of justice that still affect Jewish thought and attitudes. It touches on the classical philosophical problem of evil, while recognizing the intensity and tragedy of human loss. Chant is not merely a device to prettify Scriptures, make them easier to memorize or easier to listen. It is a signpost to interpretation. The themes and import of "The Dedication Story" should be examined in the light of its extraordinary trop.

After the redemption from slavery in Egypt and the revelation at Mount Sinai, the people of Israel, at God's behest, have built a sanctuary — the *Mishkan* — for the worship of God. It is a tabernacle designed for travel in the Wilderness, and it is resplendent. The way has not been smooth. Moses disappeared into the cloud atop the mountain for forty days. In doubt over his return, Israel made a golden calf to serve as their focus of worship. Moses' brother Aaron had been made responsible for the leadership of the people in Moses' absence. Aaron failed to direct them properly, even assisting them in the creation of the golden calf. Thousands died as a consequence. Moses finally persuaded God to forgive the people, and to continue to let His presence dwell in their midst. The shameful event now behind them, the people complete the *Mishkan* enthusiastically, *precisely* according to God's instruction of Moses. God instructs Moses on the conduct of sacrificial rites, which he is to instruct Aaron and his sons.

The stage is set for Leviticus, chapters 8-10.

"The Dedication Story"

Moses performs the dedication ritual as he has been instructed. Aaron is to be the High Priest, serving with his four sons, who will perform the duties of the ordinary priests. In dedicating the *Mishkan*, Moses finds the consecration of Aaron and his sons emotionally charged. He begins his final ritual act, the Ordination sacrifice, whose blood is to be placed on the right earlobe, thumb and great toe of Aaron and his four sons. A **Shalshelet** on the word *"And-he-slaughtered"* calls us to consider what Moses must be feeling, suggesting that he is uncertain, wavering, quaking. Doses he feel the significance of the historical moment? Is he fearful, and aware of the great peril, with premonitions of what is about to happen? Is he ambivalent and perhaps regretful about relinquishing the role of representative in Israel's service to God? The text leaves us to speculate; the trop calls attention to his moment of internal conflict. Moses completes the consecration of the priests, his ritual work done. Aaron and his sons must then spend seven days at the entrance to the sanctuary, preparing themselves for their new responsibility.

"And it came to pass on the eighth day" (Leviticus 9:1): instructed by Moses, Aaron and his sons carry out the ritual offerings of the day, in sight of all the people. The ceremony proceeds exactly "as God commanded Moses." Ritual ends in spectacle and wonder: "Moses and Aaron went into the Tent of Meeting, and came out, and blessed the people: and the glory of the Lord appeared unto all the people. And there came a fire out from before the Lord, and consumed upon the altar the burnt offering and the fat; when all the people saw, they shouted with joy, and fell on their faces." But in the very next moment: "And Nadav and Avihu, the sons of Aaron, took each his censer, and put fire therein, and put incense thereon, and offered strange fire before the Lord, which He commanded them not. And there went out fire from the Lord, and consumed them, and they died before the Lord." The chant calls attention to the confusion of the moment in highlighting the ambiguity of the word "not." Were they explicitly told not to do this, or was their act simply not commanded?

Moses searches to keep order. He has an intuitive sense of the meaning of what has just happened, as if things he has been told, premonitions, suddenly make sense.[54] He says to Aaron: "This is it that the Lord spoke, saying: 'I will be sanctified in them that are close to me, and before all the people I will be glorified.' And Aaron became silent." The Torah leaves much to the imagination of the listener, and so will I. What are the stage directions for this scene? What is Aaron voicing before he becomes silent? What is Moses' tone of voice? For Moses next utterance, the *te'amim* and the text will give us more of a hint.

Moses takes charge, but the chant suggests that he is shaken. In a wavering, fearful tone, he tells two cousins to draw near. Trop alludes to complex feelings that accompany tragedy, judgment, and destruction. The cousins are to remove the bodies of the dead from the sanctuary. Moses then tells Aaron and the two remaining sons, Elazar and Itamar, that they are to shun the usual signs of grief, and leave displays of mourning to the people. They must remain in the entrance of the Tent of Meeting, and they do as Moses commands. Moses' speech is jerky, suggesting a rattled leader, fearful that further harm will come to the priests, or even to the entire people. Is Moses uncertain whether they can be meticulous in their work and avoid complete destruction? After God forgave the Israelites for their sin of the golden calf, it was Moses who insisted to God that His presence, and not a mere angelic replacement, remain with the people. Does he feel responsible that his insistence has condemned Israel to destruction? What can possibly dispel the dread and anxiety that the events of the day must have left in their wake?

In the aftermath of tragedy, God speaks to Aaron directly for the first time in the Torah (Leviticus 10:8-11). He first tells Aaron that he and his sons are not to come to his work in the sanctuary in a drunken state. He then sets the priestly mission: "And to distinguish, between the holy and the secular. And to teach the children of Israel: all the laws, which God has spoken, to them by the hand of Moses." Richard Friedman: "It may

---

[54] The Sages were sensitive to this sense of foreboding in their well-known *Midrash* (See Rashi on Lev 10:3): "Moses said to Aaron, 'My brother, I had known that the House would be sanctified by [the death of] one close to God, and had imagined it would be by you or me. I now see that they [Nadav and Avihu] were greater than the two of us.' "

be that the significance of what Nadab and Abihu have done is the reason that the deity now addresses Aaron directly concerning the limitations and responsibilities of his family. Or perhaps we should understand this as an act of comfort from God to Aaron after his frightful loss."[55]

There is a final vignette (Leviticus 10:12-20) that brings "The Dedication Story" to a partial resolution. Moses begins with detailed instructions on how Aaron and his sons are to eat of the sacrificial portions that are theirs. He punctuates his instructions by noting explicitly that they are to be carried out "for so I have been commanded." Apparently later that day, a fretful Moses "diligently sought" answers about what had happened with the goat of a sin offering. The Hebrew, *darosh darash*, is a plain hint that he is overly concerned, micromanaging if you will. Moses is anxious and testy. He does not like what he finds out. The priestly portion of the goat had been burnt rather than eaten! Moses scolds his two nephews for failing to carry out his instructions exactly. Surely all are aware of the consequences of less than perfect attention in carrying out ritual duties. But then something surprising happens. Although not addressed by Moses, Aaron speaks out! He responds strongly, with a clear sense of command, and tells his brother why his sons had acted appropriately: "Look, today they offered their sin-offering to God, and things like these have happened to me; if I had eaten a sin-offering today, would that be good in God's eyes?"[56] The Torah concludes, "And Moses heard, and it was good in his eyes."

With this abrupt, enigmatic verse, "The Dedication Story" comes to a close. The sudden ending leaves the reader with a breathless sense: "what was that all about?"

---

[55] Friedman, *Commentary on the Torah*, p. 342

[56] The text of this "epilogue" is just a little obscure. It is not clear what sin offering is being discussed, or how exactly it was usually handled, what Moses thought was the problem, or what exactly Aaron means. I have left this part of the story vague as the Torah does. Commentators fret over the details. The Talmud will deduce that this *Chatat* offering was the New Moon sacrifice. Torah's occasional vagueness is an intentional literary device. The main point is that whatever the sacrifice, it was not performed to Moses' satisfaction.

There is no short answer to this question. The story is a richer source of wisdom and consolation than might be imagined, surprisingly "modern" and complex. It will allow us to reflect on our own spiritual needs, and how we make sense of the world. A pivotal question is the central problem that has ever confronted people of faith: the problem of suffering. As Ivan says to Alyosha in *The Brothers Karamazov*:

> Imagine you are creating a fabric of human destiny with the object of making men happy in the end, giving them peace and rest at last, but that it was essential and inevitable to torture to death only one tiny creature...and to found that edifice on its unavenged tears, would you consent to be the architect on those conditions?

This question was not a problem for the pagan world in which the religion of Israel was born. Gods were capricious and whimsical, and needed no justification. To emerge from this view to the monotheistic sense of purpose in the service of a loving Creator, death and suffering were realities that had to be confronted. There are no quick explanations, no simple philosophical answers. As always, in dealing with life's most difficult and complex issues, the Torah's strategy is "let me tell you a story."

Death and dying: consolation in the Jewish tradition

A country doctor is never far from death, and has intimate opportunities to see the variety of emotional responses in patients and families. How people handle the ultimate crisis depends on temperament, social support, and how they see the world. A religious viewpoint aims in some measure to address this need. Attending funerals of patients and friends in East Tennessee, Jewish and non-Jewish, I have watched members of my community seek consolation and try to make sense of life at a time of crisis and grief. Being steeped in tradition and community is a consistent help. I have been grateful for the solace that my own traditional practices provided after the deaths of my parents. Jewish practice, prayer, and action were central supports in my time of loss.

A commonplace truism holds that to find out about a people's religious belief, one should look at their liturgy rather than their theological writings: what do they pray? Of the many sources one could choose, I will examine two in detail, because they pertain to the question of justice and suffering in the world. First, the morning service before the central prayer "*Shema Yisrael*" begins with the blessing: "Blessed are you God, King of the universe, fashioner of light, and creator of darkness; maker of peace and creator of all there is." Second, in the burial service, is a prayer called *Tsiduk Hadin*, "Justification of the Judgment." Although the arrangements of these prayers are rabbinic in origin, they are drawn from ancient Scriptures.

I quoted the blessing before the *Shema* at the top of this Chapter. It is adapted from Isaiah 45:7, "I form light and create darkness; I make peace and create evil [or: 'destruction']." Though the word "evil" is transmuted in the liturgy to the more acceptable "all there is," the implication is the same. There is one Creator, who made not only light but also darkness. We do not turn our back on the existence of evil, of suffering, but somehow must accept it as part of the totality of creation. The *Shacharit* service will go on to dwell on the creation of light and warmth, both material and spiritual. It describes the entirety of creation as taking place through God's attribute of mercy (*rachamim*). The revelation of the Torah is seen as an act of God's love. This mindset — sensing the world as a manifestation of divine mercy and love, without turning a blind eye to the existence of evil and suffering — is the framework for approaching the central statement of the *Shema*: "Hear Israel, the Lord our God, the Lord is One." The opening blessing is a declaration of belief that in its totality the world is, somehow, right and good.

Jews reemphasize this concept at the time of death of a loved one. One memory of my father's funeral remains vivid. As we walked with the coffin to the grave, the rabbi intoned the words of *Tsiduk Hadin*, a collection of biblical verses which begins "The Rock is perfect in all His work, for all his ways are just…" It is a short prayer and highly repetitive. The words that keep echoing are:

tsedek...tsadik...tamim...rachamim...dayan...din...mishpat...
shofet...emet...yashar. Righteousness...upright...perfect...
mercy...judge...judgment...truth...correct.

I had not remembered the prayer, although many of its verses were familiar from other contexts. Was it said at my mother's funeral two years earlier? At my father's last rites I remember these words pounding like hammer blows in my head, at once terrible and a source of comfort. It was helpful that the prayer kept coming back to the metaphor of judgment, which might seem cruel at a moment of grief, but this served a purpose. It conveyed to me a sense that the order of the world is not completely disrupted, that it still makes sense. There is no avoiding death. My father's was at the end of a long and honored life, but it still felt unfair and premature. I have seen many families endure this calamity. Death often feels unfair and premature, even when there has been time to see death coming and to say goodbye, and even when it is a peaceful end to pain and hardship. I took a painful comfort from *Tsiduk Hadin.*

Reactions are more intense when death is sudden and unanticipated, even more so when the victim is young, full of life's potential. Death feels particularly tragic when the deceased is prominent and admired. The deaths of young public figures such as John Kennedy, Princess Diana, and John Lennon resulted in worldwide outpouring of grief, and a reaching out to those left behind. Such was the situation of Nadav and Avihu, young men full of promise, struck down unexpectedly at a time of public rejoicing. "The Dedication Story," with its dramatic flourishes, suggests that the response to deaths of prominent beloved young people was no less than it is today ("and your brothers, all the house of Israel, will weep for the burning, which God has burned"). The telling comes from a perspective little different from that of our current liturgy, a need to reconcile harsh events with a sense of rightness of the world. But the story is even more complex; there is more to the story than death. There is also the story of a momentous beginning. An enduring institution of great importance is being born. The meaning of the *Mishkan* is worth a closer look.

Mishkan: the tabernacle in the Wilderness and the transmission of revelation

It is first worth looking at the *Mishkan* in its "historical" context. Not the archeological history, for this is lost. A temporary structure of wood, cloth and animal skins will not leave a trace. I am concerned rather with the story as we tell it, the narrative that we carry with us in our memory.

I like to think of the Jewish Saga as having four stages:

- Origins: a formative early phase that we tell of in Genesis and the first chapters of Exodus, shrouded in the mists of time. At its conclusion, Israel is enslaved and powerless in Egypt, hanging on to a vision of redemption promised in an ancestral prophecy.

- Nationhood: This phase begins with the Exodus from Egypt, a renewal of the ancestral covenant with God, and the establishment of a unique outpost of monotheistic worship in the ancestral homeland. As in the surrounding pagan world, the predominant form of worship for Israel is a sacrificial rite in a temple, though the meaning and function of that rite has been radically transformed through Divine covenant. With a seventy-year hiatus, the Babylonian Exile, this ritual lasts for some fifteen hundred years.

- Dispersion: the Great Exile begins with the destruction of the Temple by the Roman Empire in the year 70. It will last nearly two thousand years. Cataclysm and destruction are followed by the flowering of rabbinic Judaism. Prayer in synagogue and hearth becomes the mode of worship.

- Restoration and Renewal: A new stage was ushered in yet again with tragedy and rebirth when the State of Israel was established in 1948, only three years after the Holocaust in Europe claimed the lives of one third of world Jewry.

Leviticus is set toward the start of the stage I have called Nationhood, at the foot of Mount Sinai. The revelation at Sinai is a formative moment.

Transmission of its message would require a vehicle that could endure more than a millennium in a hostile environment. That vehicle was the Temple. It is the holiest of the shrines Israel will ever use, and its most transitory — as at the revelation at Sinai, so too a the dedication of *Mishkan*, the Tabernacle in the Wilderness.

The *Mishkan* will last for the forty years of wandering in the Wilderness, and will be installed in Shilo for the early years of Israel's occupation of the land. It is a structure for nomads, designed for transport from place to place, to be taken apart and reassembled. Its blueprint is God given. At its heart in the Holy of Holies are the tablets of the Ten Commandments, housed in a gold-plated Ark whose cover incorporates sculptures of two "cheruvim,"[57] a rare piece for a religion that forbids graven images of any sort, for any purpose. The Torah tells us that the glory of God filled the *Mishkan*. It was a place where the Divine Presence was experienced directly. The medieval commentator Ramban noted the similarity between the *Mishkan* and Mount Sinai.[58] Modern scholars have elaborated on this structural similarity. The outer court of the people is similar to the foot of the mountain, both approachable by the people, but only in a state of ritual purity. The inner sanctum, the Tent of Meeting, accessible only to the priests, is like the lower reaches of the mountain. Moses, Aaron, Nadav and Avihu, and seventy elders ascended the lower reaches of Mount Sinai for a more intimate vision of God than is permitted the rest of the people. Finally, the Holy of Holies is comparable to the very top of the mountain. A cloud, the visible manifestation of God, occupies both. Only Moses can ascend to the top of the mountain, and only at the invitation of God. Only Aaron can enter the Holy of Holies, only at a certain time of the year, and only after special rituals of preparation and purification.

There is also a direct connection between the mountaintop and the Holy of Holies. It houses the tablets of the law, written by God, and

---

[57] Tradition teaches that these were winged figures with the faces of a male and a female child.

[58] Ramban, commentary on Exodus 25.

given to Moses at Sinai — both the shattered originals and God's later copy. What has been constructed in the form of a shrine is a replica of Sinai that can serve as an immediate physical reminder of the intensity of the spiritual experience. Israel's shrines over the second period of its history will be one removed from this, but will still carry a taste of the same immediacy to God. The smoke of the incense in the Temple will recall the divine cloud of Glory. The presence of a forbidden central place will serve as a reminder of contact with the most sacred: the revelation at Sinai, and the dedication of the *Mishkan*.

There was a need for a vivid constant reminder of Sinai. Biblical and archeological evidence both point to the interplay and rivalry between pagan and Israelite religions throughout the Temple period. Cautions, warnings, and extreme penalties do not keep the people from straying into cultic practices. The incompatibilities of the two perspectives don't serve as a barrier. It is not a great wonder. Mary Douglas writes of the difficulty from an anthropological point of view. Renouncing paganism in favor of the "severely monotheistic" religion of Israel involved abandoning the king as a religious figure and giving up ancestor worship, demons, magic, divination, and physical images of supernatural powers. Finding one's place in the world became a challenge:

> There were to be no more horoscopes or auguries, no auspicious times for engaging in work or war and inauspicious times for staying at home, only the one holy Sabbath day of God. Add to all this that images were banned because of their association with idolatry, and the gulf between the religion of the Bible and those of the surrounding peoples can hardly be exaggerated.[59]

The Rabbis recognized the temptation of paganism. *Midrash* tells us of a dream conversation between Rav Ashi, a Rabbinic Sage, and the wicked King Menashe of Judea. Rav Ashi could not understand why King Menashe fostered idol worship. "Had you been alive then, you would have hiked up your robes to run after me," says King Menashe.

---

[59] Douglas, *Leviticus as Literature*, p. 4

At stake for Israel as they launch their adventure at Sinai is the perpetuation of the collective memory of the Exodus and the events at Sinai, upon which the religious tradition depends. Even today, despite 3500 years of history, there are incessant cries that Judaism is doomed by this or that cultural trend. There was much more cause for anxiety about the fate of Israel in Moses' time. When God calls Moses at the burning bush to return to Egypt and rescue his people, he is reluctant. Was he afraid? Had the former Egyptian prince grown comfortable with the safe, obscure life of a shepherd? Was he, as he pleads, a poor speaker? The tales of his earlier life speak of impetuosity, courage, and an extreme inability to stand by idly while the weak are oppressed. Yet he is desperate to avoid the call. It cannot be that Moses is afraid for himself. Perhaps Moses was terrified of becoming an instrument of disaster for his people. It would not take a prophet to foresee the difficulties ahead, just a clear sense of the powers that the people would be called on to confront, of the character of a people enslaved for generations that he knew too well, and of the temptations of freedom. If so, Moses' fears proved correct. Exodus and the stand at Sinai notwithstanding, the seductiveness of idolatry was painfully brought home by the incident of the golden calf. God was on the brink of destroying the people he redeemed, until Moses' pleas for mercy carried the day. Fortunately, God had chosen the right emissary. Meanwhile, Aaron his brother, left in charge in his absence, has failed him. Who can Moses trust but himself?

Building the *Mishkan* is the ultimate sign that Israel is again in God's good graces and that the enterprise can continue. Moses carefully and personally oversees the building. Everything is done "as God commanded Moses," the refrain of the last chapters of Exodus. Moses is responsible for initiating the dedication of the *Mishkan*. But he knows that eventually he must turn the service over to his brother Aaron, whose one episode of authority was a complete disaster. By now Moses can have no doubt of the awesome power that is in their midst, of God's insistence on faithfulness to Him alone, of the consequences of breaking faith with their promise. At stake is Israel's mission in the world and its very survival. The *Mishkan* is key. Everything has to go perfectly. When it doesn't, Moses is at first uncertain where to turn.

Nadav and Avihu: why did they die? Justice in Leviticus

There are several passages in the Torah that cry out for elucidation and defy our best efforts to answer the question "Why did this happen?" These passages lead to not one interpretation, but many. A good example is the episode in Numbers 20 when Moses arouses God's ire and is told he will not enter the Promised Land. What was his sin or error? There are as many explanations as there are words in the verses. The story of Nadav and Avihu is equally perplexing. Alternative explanations for why they died abound. They brought fire from their house rather than from the altar, as they should have. They had been told not to do this (Exodus 30:9), and violated a direct commandment. They were arrogant and impatient to perform the service themselves rather than wait until their turn would come, after they succeeded their father. They acted individually, and did not consult each other. They were careless, and simply did not appreciate the hazard of approaching too close. They actually desired their fate, having had a taste at Sinai of ecstatic communion with God. They were drunk. There are textual reasons for *considering* most of the above explanations. All, except perhaps for the simple "they just got too close," have an element of fancy about them. But there is no explicit justification for any of them. The Torah simply tells us that they died at the hand of God. All the above "single-cause" explanations reflect an attempt to impose cause-and-effect type thinking on a text that works with a somewhat different logic.

Mary Douglas, citing anthropological and philosophical references, makes the point that Leviticus represents a different mode of thought than the "rational-instrumental" or "dialogic" mode of thinking that comes to dominate Western thought.[60] She sees this latter type of thinking represented well by the book of Deuteronomy and the rabbinic tradition that follows it. The thinking of Leviticus by contrast is called "analogic," reasoning less by cause and effect, and more by correlation

---

[60] Douglas, *Leviticus as Literature*, p. 13ff.

and analogy. She is careful to point out that it is not illogical, primitive, or superstitious, but rather has its own fully developed rules of reasoning. Failing to recognize this holistic mode of thought is one of the reasons we underrate the depth of the text. Douglas points out that when we try to impose dialogic processes on a text that reasons differently, we misread the text. Douglas implies that the later Jewish tradition comes to be dominated by dialogic thinkers, and that this is one of the reasons that Leviticus seems so strange to us. I would propose that Jewish thought — to this day — has integrated these two modes of thinking, and that Jews move back and forth somewhat freely in both these domains. The tension between these two modes of thought often generates questions that hover about us as we search for meaning in our stories, history, and tradition.

We demand explanations for the deaths of the two young priests. If a fire went out from God and devoured them, there must have been a just cause. But this is not the way Leviticus would have posed the question. There is no reason to think there is a single cause. Certainly none is mentioned. On the other hand, Leviticus is likely to have had some sort of framework for reconciling the deaths with the notion of a just and meaningful universe and a compassionate God. Douglas writes:

> This…story in Leviticus is about the Lord's justice in general, the very nature of Hebrew law, its symmetry and logical foundation. In a very old and self-consciously literary book, we need to find a literary level of interpretation: the story about the sons of Aaron… [is] about poetic justice, judgment in its most elementary form. The covenantal principal surfaces in these stories as a rule of reciprocity. The word for covenant is not necessarily used, but the idea of a network of balanced mutual obligation is implicit.[61]

Douglas takes a position that some traditional commentators have espoused. The deaths of the sons by burning balance Aaron's sin in helping with the building of the golden calf, also born in fire. She finds many connections and allusions between the Exodus and Leviticus

---

[61] Douglas, *Leviticus as Literature*, p. 205.

stories. She notes that Exodus states that the sins of the fathers are visited on three generations. Douglas' reading of the story is also persuasive, and yet too simplistic. I come back to her own assertion that Leviticus' major theological ideas are "God's grandeur, his unswerving justice, and unfailing compassion." It will turn out that the more complex interpretation of the Nadav and Avihu incident suggested by its trop will touch on exactly these themes.

One commentator has a view of the situation complex enough to serve as a starting point. Rabbi Chaim ibn Attar lived in Morocco and Israel in the early eighteenth century. He is better known by the name of his Torah commentary, Or Hachayim [lit. "The Light of Life"]. He states that there were three reasons for the deaths of Aaron's sons, and it was the conjunction of all three that led to their death. No two alone would have been sufficient. First, there was the matter of their coming too close to the Holy of Holies, without proper preparation and without the required invitation, as Richard Friedman also points out. Second, Aaron's sin of the golden calf had gone unpunished, as Douglas notes. Third, an example was needed. Contact with ultimate Holiness requires exact adherence to ritual, or there is danger to the entire people. The only way this would be effectively conveyed is through example: what are the consequences of improper ritual practice? The lesson would have to come through the agency of the best and the brightest, the chosen ones ("through those close to me will I be sanctified") — even these cannot escape the consequences of careless behavior.

Or Hachayim's explanation is harsh to modern sensibilities. We like to dwell on pleasant Torah passages that leave us feeling good, and to avoid discussion of passages that challenge our notions of fair play. We have found many ways to dismiss what we don't want to hear. We can regard Torah as representative of an archaic way of thinking, and imagine ourselves more sophisticated and refined. Another favorite strategy to avoid being bothered is to decide that we know who the writer is, and what his political motives were. Some critical scholars, for example, have read the "Dedication Story" and the story of the golden calf as an attempt to discredit and diminish the lineage of Aaron by a member of a rival political party. I have come to be on guard for this sort of temporal chauvinism or facile dismissal. Much more rewarding is to investigate further when the Torah seems to be giving a bothersome message. When the Torah's meaning seems hard to swallow, or conflicts with my notion of what is right, I perk up my ears and listen better. The story of Nadav and Avihu is difficult. They were *not* bad people. It is unclear whether they were given a warning *not* to do what they did. Their death did not "just happen," but came at the hand of God. How can their severe punishment be explained?

First reason: they came too near to the Sacred. When the people stood at Mount Sinai, God told Moses to warn the people a second time about approaching the mountain, lest He "break out" among them. As Friedman points out about the fate of Nadav and Avihu, this is an automatic consequence. The sense is not that God would be angry at the approach. After all, anyone approaching would likely have the best intention — to get a closer look. At Sinai, God is more concerned than Moses, who replies that he does not need to repeat the warning. God knows better. Sooner or later human curiosity will lead to testing the limits. Nothing out of bounds occurred at Sinai. The fearsome holiness of the place was enough to keep the people at bay.[62] But not so the *Mishkan*, and the psychology is plausible. The degree of majesty, the intensity of the holiness progressively declines as the people gain distance from Sinai. Sinai is holier and more awesome than the *Mishkan*, which is holier than the Temple, which is certainly more revered and sacred than a modern synagogue. The young priests' growing sense of familiarity with sacred places and rites leaves them vulnerable to just such a lapse in judgment: "If I can perform this act, then this other act is only a small step." Adornment and creativity are normal and generally positive human impulses. As in many of the Torah's stories, there is a sense of inevitability in human choices.

---

[62] Moses himself will tell us (Deut 5:5) that Israel's fear of the Divine fire on the mountain kept them from approaching.

Second reason: the death of the sons is punishment for the sin of the father. This seems reprehensible! How is it just that a person is punished for someone else's acts? We love fairness, and want desperately for the world to be fair. Will the judge of all the earth not do justice? But the Torah is realistic, and not occupied with wishful thinking. Objecting to the principle that the sins of parents are visited on their children is objecting to the nature of the world, and simple logical consequences. The daily reminders in my medical practice are painful. My child patients who grow up in homes that are abusive, or homes where the parents are involved with alcohol or drugs face daunting life problems, and some will not recover. The worst feeling is the knowledge that some of these little victims will grow up to be victimizers themselves. Three or four generations? Some families seem locked in destructive patterns well beyond that time frame. Of course some individuals will transcend these problems and put their lives together. Remember Or Hachayim's sense that no *one* reason would have been adequate to condemn the sons. Nadav and Avihu could have turned out differently had they acted differently. Their fate was also in their own hands.

There is another connection between Aaron's actions at Sinai and the death of his sons. In fashioning the golden calf, Aaron intended to create an image of the God of Israel to be worshiped, not to establish a cult of a new deity. Moses had disappeared, leaving the people leaderless. Aaron gave in to the popular demand for a visible form of worship, to help with the people's anxiety. It was not that he had led the people to worship foreign gods, but rather that he was careless about the form of worship insisted upon by the God of Israel. His transgression had gone unpunished, perhaps giving the false impression that it could not have been too bad. Aaron's laxity, modeled for all the people to see, comes back to haunt him. His children die when they commit a similar, if much lesser transgression.

Third reason: the deaths of Aaron's sons had to serve as an example. Many commentators see the pair as motivated by an excess of ardor, love, and enthusiasm — their "strange fire" an attempt at spontaneous religious expression. Or Hachayim sees them not as wicked or arrogant but as the best of the best, sincere and devoted. But they had violated a boundary, and their violation comes at a pivotal moment. If there were no consequences, it would send a message that violations of the sacred are tolerable. The central story of the revelation at Sinai requires a physical replica for effective transmission of the tradition. The earthly model must partake of the holiness of the original experience, and impart this feel successfully. The fate of the entire Israelite enterprise rests on the success of this moment, the dedication of the *Mishkan*. As Friedman commented, leaders are held to a stricter standard. And so the fate of Nadav and Avihu is sealed. They were caught in a complicated web of causation, in a set of circumstances both beyond their control and due to their own agency, at a time of critical historic importance.

But if this were the whole story, I would be disappointed. Non-Jews have a tendency to imagine the "Old Testament" as all about a wrathful God, jealous and powerful. This is far different from the actual feel of Torah, which gives equal emphasis to God's attributes of mercy and love balancing the attribute of justice. The central theme of the Exodus is God's compassion for the downtrodden and powerless. Even the story of the golden calf ends with forgiveness. Song is helpful here. Chant, as emotional amplifier, enables us to see "The Dedication Story" not as a parable about punishment for excess ardor but rather for what it is: a rich human tale, told with empathy and sensitivity.

Nadav and Avihu: compassion in tragedy

Exodus connects Israel's journey to God's purpose for mankind. There will be risk and danger throughout the millennia to those who are closest to its purpose. There is the constant need to reaffirm the mission and rededicate ourselves to it, to decide whether or not it is worth the sacrifice. Leviticus repeatedly plays with these themes in its language. Nadav and Avihu err by "drawing close." Moses tells Aaron that God will be sanctified by those who are most near. The Hebrew word for sacrifice is *lehakriv*, literally "to make close." The early steps of Israel's spiritual journey involve a dangerous closeness with the sacred. Until the people learn the rules the peril is great, just as at the start of any journey into the unknown, such as exploring a continent or venturing into outer space.

It is with tenderness and compassion for the human condition that the Torah recounts the emotional toll of tragedy on its protagonists. Their inner struggle and how they achieve mastery over it are central themes of the only story Leviticus chooses to share with us of the lives of its characters. It does so with the deft strokes of a master storyteller, whose medium is the music of chant. As Goren said of **Shalshelet**, the unusual trop of "The Dedication Story" allows us to peek into the emotional lives of our heroes. What do we find? Not stereotypical one-dimensional figures — an impervious Moses, a righteous Aaron — but humans with recognizable emotions. Like human beings in real life dealing with loss, they have to reconstitute themselves and move on with their task. They are changed in the process.

One of the things I like best about biblical tales is the remarkable depiction of its characters, the like of which will not appear on the literary scene again for thousands of years. The year 2000 saw publication of the book *From Dawn to Decadence: 500 years of Western Cultural Life, 1500 to the Present* by the historian Jacques Barzun, already then in his nineties. It is a sweeping account of the last half millennium — events, ideas, and arts. Barzun attributes the invention of "character" in literature to Montaigne and Shakespeare: "the…fact is that before Shakespeare there are no characters, only types." Montaigne in an essay "On the Inconsistency of Our Actions" pointed out the difference between a type and a character:

> The type may exhibit all kinds of tricks and tastes and gestures that make him different, recognizable, but his "stance" is unchanging, "typical." Not so in the Character. He is, as we say, many-sided, which is why we also speak of seeing someone "in the round."[63]

What looks like contradictory behavior in the Character is just the inconsistency inherent in human action, as complex creatures respond to complex situations. This is in accord with real life. The only thing that

---

[63] Barzun, *From Dawn to Decadence*, p. 135.

would surprise me at this point is having a week without being surprised at a story from my practice.

Barzun is only off a few thousand years. Biblical figures emerge as characters in the sense defined above. There are notable examples spanning the life cycle from impetuous youth to bitter old age, such as Jacob and David. We watch Judah's transformation from the irresponsible ringleader who sells his brother into the hero who offers himself as a slave in place of the new favored son, Benjamin. The Bible, like Montaigne, also recognizes that people change over time, and can alter and transcend patterns of behavior. It lays out expectations for growth and moral choice, and insists on individual responsibility. It recognizes the decline that comes to all with age.

The complexity of the Bible's depiction of character, and of humans as moral beings possessed of free will is not necessarily obvious. The Torah uses sharply limited narrative conventions. Torah will recount what a character does or says. If it depicts emotions, they are the broad, obvious kind, the ones that can be clearly read in a person's action or expression — anger, sadness, fear, love, and hatred. It rarely describes motivations. The effect is often to leave the listener guessing about nuances of feelings, or the reasons for a character's behavior. But even with these strict self-imposed rules, a vivid sense of the character of the major figures — Jacob, Joseph, or Moses, for instance — emerges from these narrative accounts.

What can we say about the characters in "The Dedication Story"? Moses is ambivalent and hesitant about relinquishing his role as ritual leader. He is shaky in the face of the sudden disaster, his uncertainty conveyed in choppy speech and in the music of the chant. In the final episode of the story, he responds with a testy, overanxious concern. Moses is trying to oversee the smallest details of the sacrificial rite. We get less of a glimpse into Aaron's internal struggle. What is Aaron all about? This is a more difficult question. There are *Midrash*im that expand on Aaron's character and exploits, and perhaps some of these were contemporaneous with the biblical text and part of the same tradition. But I would pose a different challenge: what can be gleaned about Aaron from the Torah text alone? The Torah's focus shifts to Aaron in only a few instances. Whatever can be learned of Aaron's character and growth will have to be learned from a handful of acts and utterances.

Until "The Dedication Story," Aaron has stood in Moses' shadow. It is a misreading to see Moses as slow to speak, and Aaron as eloquent, despite the apparent textual basis for this common conception of the pair. At the burning bush in Exodus 4:10, Moses claims a speech handicap as an excuse to avoid his mission, and God tells him that Aaron will be his spokesman, his "prophet." But Aaron only once speaks without Moses, in the initial address to the Israelites. He will never address Pharaoh alone. As the ten plagues unfold, Moses has no difficulty speaking for himself. Aaron serves for moral support and staff waving, and progressively retreats into the background. Prior to his consecration as High Priest in Leviticus, the golden calf episode is the main example of Aaron's leadership without Moses, and it is a fiasco. Moses expresses his harsh disapproval. Aaron's answer is feeble; he is meek and tries to evade responsibility. Unaccountably he is spared direct punishment and is still designated to carry on the sacrificial rites. He retreats further to the background. He has nothing to do with the construction of the *Mishkan*. Even when it comes time to learn the laws of the sacrificial rite, God speaks to Moses, who functions as Aaron's teacher and superior: "And God spoke to Moses, saying: 'Command Aaron and his sons, saying: 'This is the law of the *Olah*....' '" How must Aaron feel watching the swirl of activity, waiting?

At Aaron's consecration, he remains passive. Moses dresses him in priestly garments, and anoints him with the sacred oil. It is Moses who performs the three sacrifices, and ordains Aaron and his sons with the blood of the second ram. Then Aaron and his sons sit in watch at the opening of the Tent of Meeting for a week. Through all this, nothing suggests what is going through Aaron's mind. On the eighth day, Aaron's priestly work begins. Moses is still present, telling Aaron how to proceed. When Aaron gives the people the first of his priestly blessings, Moses is at his side. Together, they give a joint benediction. And then — tragedy.

We have not heard Aaron speak since the episode of the golden calf, and must wonder what it means when we are told that he "became silent" after the deaths of his children. He has been silent for some time. Silence is powerful. It leaves no clue to what is going on internally, and others are left to imagine the internal state. One can conceive of Aaron's silence as passive or as an active withholding of self, leaving Moses without support. In this silence, an extraordinary event occurs. For the first time God addresses Aaron directly. The content of this encounter is both warning and reassurance: do not come to the work of the sanctuary intoxicated, and you will not die. Further (Lev 10:10-11):

> And to separate: between the sacred and the profane, and between the impure and the pure. And to teach the Children of Israel: all the laws, which God spoke to them at the hand of Moses.

It is likely that even in ancient Israel, there was the same sense about divine communication that has been expressed by two thousand years of rabbinic tradition. The Torah uses language of "speech" to indicate revelation, though what actually happens in such a moment remains a mystery. This is suggested here in the fragmentary language of the last two verses, which I have duplicated in the translation. There is intimation that God conveys a comprehensive and broad picture of the priestly role for ages to come, of the essence of the concepts that the ritual embodies.

Our story then concludes with the episode about the sin offering. In that passage, Moses betrays his continued anxiousness, Aaron finds his voice: "Look, today they offered their sin-offering to God, and things like these have happened to me; if I had eaten a sin-offering today, would that be good in God's eyes?" Much is packed into very spare narrative detail. Aaron's boldness and confidence are clear in this one-line quote. Rashi, the preeminent medieval commentator, recognizes assertiveness in Aaron's remark, which begins, "And Aaron spoke (*Vayedaber*) to Moses" instead of "And Aaron said (*Vayomer*)." He comments that this is a sign of intense, strong (*az*) language. And so it is. There is irritation and challenge in his words. They stand in sharp contrast to Aaron's reply when Moses came down from the mountain and chastised him about the Golden Calf (Exodus 32:22). There Aaron begins obsequiously, "Let my Lord not be angry..." and goes on to give a feeble excuse — the people and not he were responsible for the idol.

This is a changed Aaron — now confident in himself and his role, a difference convincing and recognizable. How the change occurs is hinted at, but not explicitly told. Is there recognition of personal responsibility, recollection of past sins? Does it come from a sense of grief at a great loss? Does it follow from the combination of tragic loss, followed by a direct and comforting communication from God? Is it plausible? Would the direct communication of the mission for the ages not change a person? Like many of the Torah's stories, Aaron's transformation is a surprise. It could be taken as out of character for Aaron, but this ignores the Torah's conception of human character. Its heroes are multidimensional, their actions not always predictable. Aaron's confidence and forcefulness may be unexpected from what we have seen of him previously, but fits well with the Torah's view of people as capable of transcending their limitations.

This last vignette brings a final resolution to the "Dedication Story." The central concern of this vignette is the interaction between the two brothers. Even before the deaths of Aaron's sons, Moses had reason to be anxious about his brother's performance in the role of High Priest. How would Aaron be affected by his ordination and the tragedy that accompanied it? Aaron's one-line reply speaks for the necessary internal change. He shows confidence in taking charge of the ritual aspects of Israelite life. He is no longer Moses' passive assistant, and is able to share the duties of leading the people. Moses is not as alone. Aaron has redeemed in some measure his conduct at the time of the golden calf, where passive acquiescence rather than leadership is the theme. He shows ability to think clearly and calmly at a time of great stress, and to go on with his duties, as Moses knows he must. And his language shows an acceptance of the will of God, and a willingness to serve even after the death of his sons. This last notion — accepting the world as it is and moving on — remains a continuing theme in Jewish accommodation to the reality of death. Moses recognizes the change in Aaron, now an equal partner as High Priest and religious leader. It is a welcome change. "And Moses heard; and it was good in his eyes."

Empathetic depiction of character in "The Dedication Story" is how Torah expresses the Creator's deep compassion for his creatures. In the short work *When Bad Things Happen to Good People*, Harold Kushner discusses one of the great truths about consolation, which has served me well in my capacity as rural doctor and counselor to my patients at times of stress and loss. Generally what a person needs at such a time is not a quick fix, some simple explanation that makes everything right. What a mourner needs is to be heard, to tell his or her story. The role demanded of one who would bring comfort is simply to listen. When things have fallen apart, we crave understanding and kinship. And so the Torah breaks in its account of the laws of holiness to tell us a story — a story of two brothers, of immense responsibilities and their tragic consequences, of rising above grief and moving on. It is a story with artful depiction of internal turmoil, told with music. In its sensitivity to its human characters Torah reveals its — and God's — immense compassion and love for His creatures, and appreciation for their heroic struggles.

In the end, this initial offering in what I hope will be an ongoing contribution to thinking about Torah chant turned out quite different than what I had intended. Edited out was a more comprehensive look at chant in favor of focusing mainly on a relatively "obscure" tale in Leviticus, and on rare trop, rather than the day to day ways in which chant transforms text. Torah's narrative art, the complexity of its conception of humans and their place in the universe, God's fairness and immense sympathy for His creatures all emerge in the chanting. Over millennia, *Midrash* has found ways of tapping into Torah to speak to each generation, to find guidance and comfort in navigating the difficulties of a perilous world. The music of the chant can serve as a fruitful tool for *Midrash*, which modern readers and listeners can use to explore the wisdom and transformative capacity of an ancient text. The story of Moses, Aaron and his sons, and the dedication of the *Mishkan*, is just one of many examples of the power of Torah unloosed in chant.

Epilogue

The past years have been a long journey for me. Writing has led to the thrill of discovery and enhanced the joy of practicing an ancient art form in a modern time. It is now over five years since I have returned to East Tennessee from my Sabbatical in New York. I am immersed in the adventures of my now grown children, the problems of my patients, the challenge of building a practice and the complex issues confronting my community. I am a different person than the passionate *ba'al keri'ah*, who ended his idyll with daily Passover Torah reading in Jerusalem.

Where I am now is a preoccupation — my family might say obsession — with the future of the world. How can we apply technology to solving problems, while remaining attentive to ancient wisdom? Karen Armstrong in *The Great Transformation: The Beginning of Our Religious Tradition* opens, "Perhaps every generation believes that it has reached a turning point of history, but our problems seem particularly intractable and our future increasingly uncertain."[64] She suggests that it is appropriate to turn for inspiration to the sages of the "Axial Age," the time of origin of Greek philosophy, monotheism in Israel, Buddhism, and Chinese thought. Armstrong contends that the spiritual insights of this age have never been surpassed. She is not alone. Thomas Friedman in *The World is Flat* writes, "When I raised this issue and the broad themes of my book with my religious teacher, Rabbi Tzvi Marx from Holland, he surprised me by saying that the flat world I was describing reminded him of the Tower of Babel."[65] I too hear echoes of the Internet in the innocent yet ominous opening of this myth: "And the whole world was one language, and only a few words...." Rabbi Marx heard the Tower of Babel story as a cautionary tale about overweening pride, and what happens when a monumental edifice is constructed without regard for its end. This ancient myth resonated in a radically different time.

---

[64] Karen Armstrong, Karen Armstrong, *The Great Transformation: The Beginning of Our Religious Tradition*.

[65] Thomas Friedman, *The World is Flat A Brief History of The Twenty-first Century*.

I agree with Armstrong's sense that mankind is at a critical juncture of history and that this is not merely the usual illusion of every era. The entire world is connected in an unparalleled fashion, with instant communication and rapid travel around the globe. There are trade connections between virtually all nations. Human destructive power has increased to the point of being able to annihilate all the higher life forms on earth. Human environmental impact has never been greater. A hole in the ozone layer, melting of arctic ice caps, depletion of the ocean's fisheries, diminishing frog populations (consider the metaphor of the canary in the mine), and extinction of species due to human impact on habitat represent problems not previously confronted on a planetary scale. Human survival and preservation of the richness of life on earth are at stake. Humans have confronted complex issues in imaginative ways, but for many of us a blind faith in technological solutions seems part of the problem. The myths of the Tower of Babel and of the Unsinkable Titanic come to mind.

There are true stories that are also parables and myths. In December 2003 an enormous underwater earthquake near Sumatra in the Indian Ocean gave rise to a tsunami, which devastated nearby coastal areas to the east. It was the worst natural disaster in my lifetime. A tsunami raced westward as well. On a group of islands off the Indian coast, Nicobar and Andaman Islands, there were small tribes who had been sheltered from development and preserved their aboriginal culture and lifestyle. There was no way to protect or warn them of the upcoming disaster. When satellite photos were analyzed in the aftermath of the disaster, the tribes were seen gathering belongings and livestock and moving inland to high ground. There was no loss of life among the indigenous people. A tribal leader later told an anthropologist their traditional teaching: when there is a great earthquake, the sea will rise. The Indian author Madusmee Matturjee was quoted by the BBC: "The aboriginals have an island survival strategy that they have developed through the knowledge of the generations." As *Scientific American* editorialized, ancient wisdom had trumped modern technology.

Jews know the secret of *their* survival over the ages. When we conclude each portion of the Torah, the person called for the *aliyah* recites: "Thank you God, King of the universe, who has given us a Torah [a Teaching] of truth, and planted eternal life in our midst." The Sages who composed this blessing taught "Turn it and turn it, for everything is in it." Oppressed, exiled, and dispersed, they retained their belief in their future, in God's love for His people, and in their mission in the world. Torah was their source of wisdom and strength.

To some it may seem that the mission of calling out an ancient work runs counter to humanity's task in the world today. It comes from another era, one of kings and tribal rulers, of slavery, of animal sacrifice, of polygamy and limited roles for women. Have we not moved on to a more advanced morality? Torah speaks of calamity as Divine punishment for sin. Surely, as sophisticated moderns we no longer accept such a simplistic outlook. And what about the Holocaust — has that not changed our awareness of these ideas forever? Torah is the possession of a people who spoke of being chosen by the Creator of the universe. Is this notion not particularistic and divisive? I have to admit that these ideas are not foreign to me. I would have argued them forcefully during my own college years.

Singing Torah and life experiences have moved me to a renewed appreciation of the Hebrew Scriptures. They are much more intricate than the above critique would suggest. Torah is a work from the period of slavery that is at its heart uncomfortable with one human being serving another. Its kings were warned to be bound by the law and not to have "their heart rise above *their brothers.*" Mary Douglas emerged from her analysis of the dietary and sacrificial laws of Leviticus with the sense that it was the expression of a "modern religion," founded on principles of justice and compassion. It is true that the Torah teaches that Israel was chosen by God for a special role in the world, but it also teaches that Abraham and his descendants are to be a "blessing" to all the people of the world, and that they are to follow paths of justice and the untranslatable *tzedakah*, which can be seen as righteousness, charity, and social justice rolled into one. At the midpoint of our annual cycle we encounter the Torah portion in Leviticus that begins "You shall be holy, for I the Lord your God am holy." We immediately follow this reading with the prophetic portion from Amos: "Are you not like the children of the Cushites to me, you children of Israel?" affirming God's providence over all nations.

I am baffled now that I ever conceived the Torah's morality as simplistic. Torah has a complex sense of the web of causation in the world, and wrestles with questions of good and evil, suffering and loss, in sophisticated ways. Stories and myths are literary means of grappling with complicated human issues that cannot be fully resolved through rational analysis. We are left with paradox, and this is as appropriate in the spiritual realm as it is in the physical. Light is both a particle and a wave. All is foreseen, destiny operates, and yet there is free will. God's acts at times seem harsh; but we still declare that He is just in all his ways and loving in all his deeds. For a full appreciation of the Torah's vision, regard Torah as a fractal. Step back and look at the whole. The progression from Noah to Abraham to Moses reflects an evolving religious consciousness of the balance of God's justice and mercy in dealing with humans. Or take a look at a detail, like the tenderness of the depiction of Abraham in his argument with God, or sensitivity in telling the deaths of Aaron's sons.

Torah is deep ancient wisdom. Chant is the voice of that wisdom, perhaps its most primal voice. The Onge tribe of Little Andaman Island preserves an oral tradition that taught how to survive a tidal wave. Torah teaches survival strategies for the world of today, no less than for the world of its origins. It reaches out to the human spirit on many levels and through the use of all human faculties, in word but also in music. Chant adds layers of liveliness and emotional richness to text. The grammar of *Te'amei Hamikra* insures fidelity of interpretation over time and across cultures. It is as if the music of the chant can blow away the layers of dust — millennia of interpretation and preconceptions — to gain access to the plain text and bring it to life, so that listeners in every age can hear it with fresh ears, with their own ears.

It is fortunate that Torah chant, as it has evolved over the years, still provides a pleasurable performing and listening experience. Sheer sound pleasure interacts with intellectual satisfaction. The emotional effect of storytelling amplifies and enriches ethical and philosophical concepts. Intuition and reason harmonize. For me the experience of calling out Torah has been integrative. I can be comfortable in my skin as a religious being, and as a country doctor aware of both scientific ideas and of the vastness and miracle of God's universe and human society.

There is potential in all religions for a pernicious destructiveness generated by a sense of superiority over other religions. This is not what I experience in Torah. Torah, like Chinese thought with its Yin/Yang mandala, is about balancing polarities. Good does not eradicate evil but is to rule over it. Justice is to be balanced by mercy. Fear and awe are balanced by love, and vice versa. Particularism and regard for one's own clan coexist with regard for all people. Genesis describes the actions not of one people's God, but the Creator of the universe. All are descended from a common ancestor. God chooses Abraham so that he may be a blessing and example to the world. His descendants must learn concern for the powerless and oppressed by going through the experience of slavery. They are to love not only their neighbor, but also the stranger as themselves. Of course the Torah dwells on the tales and laws of a particular people. It is our story, designed to teach us about our particular place in the world. It should not be read as an expression of ethnic superiority.

The Sages teach that Torah was given us to refine us, to challenge us to be our best. Jewish scholars, coming at the text from diverse perspectives, have shared the sense that this ancient document bears important messages for our time. Rabbi S.R. Hirsch, founder of Modern Orthodoxy, declared that his purpose in writing a commentary on the Torah was "to show that a unified spirit permeates the whole of the Torah and that its underlying ideas are not those of an antiquated past, but have a vital bearing on the problems and endeavors of each epoch in the history of mankind." Buber and Rosenzweig hoped that their translation would help "renew the dialogue between Heaven and Earth."

Richard Friedman, representative of modern biblical criticism, speaks of the urgency of listening to the Torah's message of caring for the natural and human world.

I am proud to claim connection to a long line of singer/storytellers who have presented ancient Teaching to the Jewish people in public chanting. My aim is to reach the hearts and minds of my listeners, giving a performance that holds the listener, and creates the same kind of pleasure as does a concert or a play. I want my audience to feel the thrill of words set to music, but my purpose is not to enthrall or blind. I strive for the ideal that musical insights be examined by the sensible and rational mind for their validity and value. I want an integration of love and fear, of ardor and caution. I try to balance decisiveness and confidence with humility and awe before the magnitude and sanctity of the task.

I am thankful to those who have accompanied me this far on the journey. I am grateful for my gifts, internal and external, that have made me the *ba'al keri'ah* I am today, and for finding venues to exercise my skills. This is not the end of the adventure. It is the middle of a long story stretching far behind us and extending into the distant future. Jewish observance pays homage to the never-ending nature of the way. "It is not placed upon you to finish the work, nor are you free to refrain from it," is a favorite teaching. The annual cycle of Torah reading concludes in the fall on the holiday *Simchat Torah*, the Rejoicing over the Law. As soon as we finish reading the last words of Deuteronomy — "… before the eyes of all Israel" — we take out another scroll and begin again, "When in the beginning God created the heavens and the earth.…" And when we finish each of the Five Books in the yearly reading, we conclude with a communal shout echoed by the *ba'al keri'ah*. It is an expression of satisfaction with the accomplishment, but also a prayer for renewal of strength during the voyage ahead:

Chazak, chazak, venit'chazek!

GLOSSARY

This glossary is an interpretation of Hebrew terms for the reader who may be unfamiliar with them. It is intended to convey what these words mean to me personally — my private internal dictionary if you will.

Aliyah (pl aliyot)

Lit. "going up." When the Torah is read publicly, the reading is divided into 3-7 portions, called *aliyot*, the number depending on the occasion. A member of the congregation is honored by being called to "go up" to the Torah and pronounce a blessing before and after the portion is read. This honor is also called an *aliyah*, as in "Which *aliyah* did you get?"

Ashkenazi

I have used the terms *Ashkenazi* (German/Eastern European) and *Sephardic* (literally "Spanish") used to describe a division of modern Jewry into two major parts. The division of the Roman Empire into Roman and Byzantine portions, followed by the split between areas under Christian and Moslem control produced a political barrier between these two worlds that separated them to some degree. In the Medieval world, the large Jewish communities of Germany and Spain, lacking ongoing, significant contact, developed in different directions. The separation widened as Ashkenazi Jewry moved eastward from Germany to Poland and farther east as a result of persecutions, while Sephardic Jewry was subjected to the Inquisition and scattered to the four winds in 1492, most notably to North Africa and other adjoining Moslem, predominately Arabic-speaking areas. This separation was never complete, and there are more similarities than differences between these two branches of Judaism. Today Jews from European background are commonly referred to as "*Ashkenazi*," Jews from Arabic lands as "*Sephardic*," or "Oriental" (in Hebrew, *edot hamizrach*).

Ba'al keri'ah

Lit. "master of recitation." Variation — *ba'al korei*. This is the term used to designate the person who chants the Torah in a public reading, and/or a person with this skill.

Chumash

The Five Books of Moses collected together in one volume or a unified set of five volumes, with commentary, sometimes with a translation. See Bibliography for description of a few of the many editions available.

Davening

The *Ashkenazi* mode of prayer, with its unique fusion of *keva* [fixed ritual] and *kavanah* [intention, concentration]. The verb form is "to *daven*." Like the word for synagogue (see *Shul*), its colloquial quality reflects a kind of intimate familiarity and comfort. *Davening* is simple to learn, but it takes years of practice to master this meditative art.

Devar Torah

"A word of Torah." Any talk using Torah text as a departing point, whether to explore content more deeply or extend lessons to one's contemporary world. As Ben Bag Bag says in Pirkei Avot (*Ethics of the Fathers*, a tractate of *Mishna*), "Turn it and turn it, for everything is in it."

Gabbai (pl gabba'im)

A community functionary whose title reflects his original function — to collect charity and the community's internally imposed financial obligations. As the synagogue was the center of the community, the gabbai's activities encompassed synagogue duties as well. Today, the function of gabbaim has become limited to the synagogue, where they carry out a range of ritual duties, most prominently, overseeing the reading of the Torah— rolling the Torah scrolls to the correct place ahead of time, assigning *aliyot*, calling up those honored with an *aliyah,* as well as, most critically, following the Torah reader and correcting errors made in the course of the reading.

Haftarah (pl haftarot)

A portion drawn from the Prophets, the middle division of *Tanakh*, read after the conclusion of the weekly Sabbath or Holiday Torah reading. It connects in theme with either the *parashah* or with the holiday cycle.

Leyn

Yiddish verb meaning to chant the Torah in public. It can be conjugated naturally in "Yinglish:" I *leyn*; I *leyned*; I am *leyning*.

Midrash (pl. Midrashim, adj. Midrashic)

A complicated word with different meanings in different contexts. Rabbi Mark Greenspan suggests in a recent Haggadah: "It is easier to see a *Midrash* than to define it. *Midrash* is both a type of literature… and a particular approach to the reading of scripture. In its largest sense, *Midrash* is the quest to find new meanings in a sacred text." I sometimes use it to mean "classical *Midrash*," collections of rabbinic explication, commentary and elaboration of biblical text roughly contemporaneous with the Mishna and Talmud (200 B.C.E.-500 C.E.)

Mishnah

The first definitive collation of the legal portions of the "Oral Torah." Set in its final form by Rabbi Judah Hanasi in about the year 200 C.E., it represents the collective discussions and opinions of rabbinical academies over the prior three hundred years.

Parashah (pl parashiyot, possessive — parashat)

I have used this term exclusively to denote the division of the Five Books of Moses into weekly readings. Each *parashah* takes its name from its first significant word. The Hebrew name for each of the five Books (for example Genesis is called *Bereishit*) is simply the name of its first *parashah*. The Hebrew word *parashah* is also used to denote the Torah scroll's traditional division into "pericopes," the technical name for the paragraphs into which the text in the Torah scrolls is *The Torah: A Modern Commentary* divided.

Shabbat (Yiddishized version: Shabbes; plural shabbatot)

The Jewish Sabbath, a day of rest coming at the end of the workweek. The essence of Jewish thought is contained in observing *Shabbat*. Commemorating the end of God's work of creation, it serves as a reminder that human life and work need to aim towards a spiritual end. By instituting a day of rest, we are also reminded of our freedom and the redemption from Egyptian bondage. Gratitude and social responsibility become themes. A day of contemplation, rest, and peace is also a foreshadowing of the time to come when the human experience is less troubled and strife-ridden. At the central point of the morning service on this holiest of our celebrations, we sing the Torah.

Shabbat Nachamu

Literally, "The Sabbath of 'Comfort ye…' " This is name given the first Shabbat after the fast day of the *Tisha B'Av*, the ninth day of the month of Av, which commemorates events of agony and loss in Jewish history, most notably the destruction of the Temple in Jerusalem and the beginning of Exile. It is one of several *Shabbatot* that takes its name from the Haftarah reading for the day. For three weeks prior to the fast day, *Haftarot* have consisted of prophecies warning of the upcoming destruction. They culminate on *Shabbat Chazon* — the Sabbath of "The Vision…" — with reading the beginning of Isaiah. *Shabbat Nachamu* launches seven weeks of readings of prophecies of comfort for the exiled people. This is one of many examples of the way the weekly readings from Torah and Prophets color and give emotional tone to the yearly cycle, augmenting the annual holidays.

Shul

The informal word Jews use for synagogue, as in "*Nu*, so who did you see in *shul* today?" Its colloquial feel accurately reflects a Jew's sense of informal comfort in his place of worship, a different feel than words like church, synagogue, temple, shrine. The derivation from the German word for school connects with the critical importance of the *shul* as an educational institution in Jewish life.

Sephardic

See Ashkenazi.

Talmud

The Talmud includes the *Mishnah*, and a much longer compilation of the discussions and commentaries on *Mishnah* in academies of study over the next three hundred years, roughly 200-500 C.E. There are two versions of this multi-volume work: The Land of Israel produced the Jerusalem *Talmud*, and the sages of the Diaspora the much more studied Babylonian *Talmud*. It is the definitive intellectual and spiritual nexus of Judaism to this day. It is a veritable fountain of disputations and divergent views. Besides legal material *Talmud* also includes anecdotes and *Midrash* — biblical legends and commentary.

Tanakh

The Hebrew Bible, the Hebrew Scriptures. It is an acronym that draws its name from its three divisions: *Torah, Nevi'im* [Prophets], and *Ketuvim* [Writings]. "Prophets" consists of the histories, Joshua through Kings; the later prophets — Isaiah, Jeremiah, Ezekiel; and the twelve "minor" prophets. "Writings" consists of Psalms, Proverbs, Job, the Five Scrolls (Song of Songs, Ruth, Lamentations, Ecclesiastes, Esther), Daniel, Ezra, Nehemiah, Chronicles. Only some of these have prescribed public reading in chant — a relatively small chunk of Prophets (see *Haftarah*) and the Five Scrolls; but all have chant indications in a Masoretic *Tanakh*. The tunes used for the various books are different. There is one tune for Torah, another for prophets. There is one for Song of Songs, Ruth, and Ecclesiastes, and a different one for Esther. The tune for Lamentations is somber and dirgelike. All the tunes are related musically, and follow the same structural rules with three exceptions. Psalms, Proverbs, and Job, commonly called the "*Emet*[66] books" after their initial Hebrew letters, look like they have the same Masoretic accents as the other "twenty-one books," but clearly have a musical/grammatical system

---

[66] Emet also means "truth" in Hebrew.

that operates with a different logic. The tradition for singing these books was lost in antiquity. I sometimes refer to the *Tanakh* minus the three *Emet* books as "the twenty one books." This presumes that we count Samuel, Kings, and Chronicles as one rather than two books, although for length considerations they are traditionally divided in two in both Hebrew and Christian bibles. This also counts the twelve "minor prophets" as one book.

Tikkun (from the Hebrew root "to fix")

An indispensable tool for the *ba'al keri'ah*. This book has the same text from the Torah in two columns on each page. The column on the left has the text as it appears in the scroll to be chanted aloud in public. The column on the right has the identical text with the addition of Masoretic vowel indications and chant accents [*te'amim*]. The *ba'al keri'ah* learns the portion to be recited on the right side, and then attempts to transfer this knowledge to the left side.

Torah

The Pentateuch, first five books of the Jewish or Christian Bible. Every synagogue has one or more copies of this work, written by hand on parchment scrolls up to three feet tall, housed in an *Aron Kodesh* or Holy Ark at the front of the sanctuary. In *Ashkenazi* synagogues, The Torah scroll has an ornate cover, and a silver breastplate and crown. Each of the wooden posts on which the scroll is wound is referred to as *etz chayim*, or "tree of life," from the liturgical verse "it is a tree of life for them that hold fast to it." In *Sephardic* synagogues the Torah scroll is housed in an equally ornamental casing. When taken out for public readings, a Torah scroll is paraded through the synagogue with song and pageantry, before it is placed at rest on a table facing or in the middle of the congregation.

Yad (literally "hand") (plural yadot)

The pointer which the Torah reader uses to indicate the text he/she is reading. While there are abstract modern pointers available today, the traditional *yad* terminates in a hand. *Yadot* have been the subject of creativity and craft over the ages, and examples can be found in many museums of Jewish artifacts. My personal *yad* is a creation of the artist Dafna Robinson, made of wood with a stone inlay with just the right heft and feel.

ANNOTATED BIBLIOGRAPHY

Chumashim — a biased view

Besides hearing the chanted Torah in synagogue readings, the *Chumash* is the main way most Jews will encounter their fundamental work. The name derives from the Hebrew word *chamesh*, "five," and it denotes the Five Books of Moses, often with translation, and virtually always with commentary. Most synagogue goers will follow along with the chanted reading in a *Chumash*. How one hears the text will be colored greatly by the tone of the translation and the perspective of the commentary. There is now a great variety of *Chumashim* among which to choose. Here are a few of the more readily available, with brief reviews.

Chumashim — general editions

The Chumash, The Stone Edition. The Art Scroll Series. Brooklyn, NY: Mesorah Publications, 1994.

> Very traditional. Strength is esthetic presentation and very extensive referencing of classical commentators and Talmudic *Midrash*. Weakness is very extensive referencing of classical commentators and Talmudic *Midrash*. Even within the range of traditional rabbinic opinion, Art Scroll tends to select commentaries that minimize the ambiguity and richness of the text in favor of a moralistic certainty.

Etz Hayim. New York: Jewish Publication Society, 2001.

> The new Conservative *Chumash*. New JPS translation (1985). Text includes straightforward and homiletic commentary on each page, and there are impressive essays on many aspects of Torah by a formidable array of contemporary scholars at the end.

Dr. J.H. Hertz, ed. The Pentateuch and Haftorah. USA: Jewish Publication Society, 1937.

> Included here because it has been the standard Chumash at Conservative synagogues for generations. Rabbi J.H. Hertz was

Chief Rabbi of England. The translation features a lot of "thee"s and "thou"s and is uncomfortable to modern ears without the elegance of the King James Version. The commentary is personal and generally insightful, but at times seems interested in cleaning up the rougher edges of Torah for a polite British audience.

Gunther Plaut, ed. *The Torah: A Modern Commentary.* New York: Jewish Publication Society, 1981.

This Chumash is the Reform movement contribution, edited by the scholar Gunther Plaut and first published in 1981. Like *Etz Hayim*, it also uses the JPS translation. Conservative and Orthodox readers might be surprised at the respect accorded traditional interpretation, although critical scholarship is accented. My favorite part of this Chumash is the interspersing of sections called "Gleanings" from varied sources, ranging from classical *Midrash* and Talmudic law to modern writers — Jewish and non Jewish.

The Rev. Dr. A. Cohen, ed. *The Soncino Chumash.* The Whitefriars Press, 1947.

The Soncino is my favorite traditional Chumash, featuring "An Exposition Based on Classical Jewish Commentaries." For the non-Hebrew speaker, it provides good "digest" of the works of the major commentators from Rashi (twelfth century) through Sforno (sixteenth century).

Chumashim — personal editions

English Chumashim

As a group these are marvelous tributes to their authors' passion for Torah. They differ from the above Chumashim in being the work of a single individual, both commentary and translation. Particularly striking is the attention each gives to its translation priorities: Alter to literary esthetics without compromising precision, Fox to authenticity to the feel of the Hebrew, Friedman to precision and "balance," and Hirsch to rendering complexities of meaning that he sees as inherent in the text. By dint of being the work of persons rather than committees, all the translations have more spice than the "general" Chumashim. I enjoy giving them greater prominence than their distribution would indicate.

Alter, Robert. *The Five Books of Moses: A Translation with Commentary.* New York: W. W. Norton and Company, 2004.

> English only. The translation takes on the admittedly impossible task of correcting what is "seriously wrong with all the familiar English translations…. Broadly speaking, one may say that in the case of the modern versions, the problem is a shaky sense of English and in the case of the King James Version, a shaky sense of Hebrew." The results (a personal opinion) are consistently fine, and sometimes magic. My main reservation is his willingness to depart from the Masoretic punctuation in the translation. The commentary is designed to give the reader a deeper understanding of the workings of the Hebrew original than can be conveyed in translation. The essay in the Introduction, "The Bible in English and the Heresy of Explanation," reproduced from Alter's earlier fragment *Genesis*, is worth the price of the book.

Fox, Everett. *The Five Books of Moses.* New York: Schocken Books, 1995.

> Fox explicitly pays homage to Buber and Rosenzweig's magnum opus of German translation. Alter recognizes its uniqueness in the introduction to his own translation: "his English has the great virtue of reminding us…of the strangeness of the Hebrew original, but it does so at the cost of often being not quite English." Fox is explicitly uninterested in Friedman's "balance," liberating himself to convey Hebrew wordplay in ways otherwise unreachable. As Alter points out, it is not always readable English, but it does occasionally achieve fine esthetics, especially read aloud.

Friedman, Richard. *Commentary on the Torah.* San Francisco: HarperSanFrancisco, 2001.

> Friedman suggests his commentary will surprise those who know

his biblical studies in its regard for Torah as a unified literary opus. His translation is in some ways the most colloquial and readable, without losing the taste of the Hebrew. I have found passages (see Chapter 8, for example) where I felt Friedman alone was willing to trust the Torah's Hebrew to speak for itself. My best tribute to this sleeper among Chumashim is extensive use of Friedman's translation, comments, and reflections in this book.

Hirsch, Rabbi S.R. Hirsch, *Commentary on the Torah.* London: The Judaica Press, 1966.

The English translation of Hirsch's nineteenth century German work is by his grandson Isaac Levy. Hirsch rejected Reform and Critical approaches to Torah, and set out to explain the biblical text "out of itself." Of his five stated aims, quoted in the "Introduction to the First English Edition," the last is shared by all who love Torah: "To show that a unified spirit permeates the whole of the Torah and that its underlying ideas are not those of an antiquated past, but have a vital bearing on the problems and endeavors of each epoch in the history of mankind."

Hebrew Chumashim

Mikraot Gedolot.

This is the term used for any of dozens of editions of Masoretic text of the Bible, surrounded by a host of commentaries. At a minimum, *Mikra'ot Gedolot* includes the following major classical commentaries:

- Targum Onkelos (Aramaic translation, but also somewhat of a commentary)

- Rashi (11th century)

- Ibn Ezra (12th century)

- Rashbam (12th century)

- Ramban (13th century)

- Sforno (15th century)

At least these are the main ones in my one-volume version. Many also include *Siftei Chachmim*, a gloss on Rashi, which clarifies obscure points, and often asks what worried the great commentator to the point that he felt a need to remark on a particular verse. More typical are five-volume publications of *Mikra'ot Gedolot* on Torah only, with an even more comprehensive set of commentators. I love this standard widely disseminated format. It represents a several-thousand-year dialogue with ancient texts.

Umberto Cassuto, *Torah, Nevi'im, Ktuvim*. Israel: Yavneh Publishing House, 1962.

This is an interesting and underused work, in the name of the Italian biblical scholar/historian Umberto Cassuto, who left his native Florence to assume a chair of Biblical Studies at the Hebrew University in Jerusalem in 1939. When I lived in Israel, it was an almost guaranteed bar mitzvah gift for a boy in public religious school. It comprises the entire *Tanakh* with Hebrew commentary, generally very straightforward, citing both traditional and modern views. It is useful in clearing up obscure Hebrew meanings, and translating archaisms into Modern Hebrew. Cassuto's love of biblical geography and archeology shines in his work.

Other Sources

Alter, Robert. *The Art of Biblical Narrative*. United States: Basic Books, 1981.

Alter, Robert. *The Art of Biblical Poetry*. United States: Basic Books, 1985.

Armstrong, Karen. *The Great Transformation: The Beginning of Our Religious Tradition*. Alfred A. Knopf e-book, ISBN 978-0-375-41317-9, 2006.

Avenary, Hanoch. *The Ashkenazy Tradition of Biblical Chant between 1500 and 1900 — Documentation and Musical Analysis.* Tel Aviv: 1978.

Barzun, Jacques. *From Dawn to Decadence: 500 Years of Western Cultural Life — 1500 to the Present.* New York: HarperCollins, 2000.

Buber, Martin and Rosenzweig, Franz, translated by Lawrence Rosenwald with Everett Fox. *Scripture and Translation.* Bloomington, Indiana: Indiana University Press, 1994.

Cohen, Miles. "The System of Accentuation in the Hebrew Bible." Undergraduate thesis, University of Minnesota, 1969.

Douglas, Mary. *Leviticus as Literature.* New York: Oxford University Press, 1999.

Friedman, Richard. *The Bible with Sources Revealed: A New View into the Five Books of Moses.* San Francisco: HarperSanFrancisco, 2003.

Friedman, Thomas. *The World is Flat A Brief History of The Twenty-first Century* (2005; expanded edition 2006; revised edition 2007), Farrar, Straus, & Giroux, New York.

Gellis, Maurice and Gribetz, Dennis. *The Glory of Torah Reading.* New Jersey: M.P. Press, 1989.

Goren, Zechariah. *Te'amei Hamikra Kefarshanut* [Trop as Exegesis]. Israel: Hakibbutz Hameuchad Publishing House, 1995.

Hoffman, Joel. *In the Beginning: A Short History of the Hebrew Language.* New York: New York University Press, 2004.

Jacobson, Joshua. *Chanting the Hebrew Bible, The Art of Cantillation.* Philadelphia, Pennsylvania: The Jewish Publication Society, 2002.

Leibowitz, Nehama. *New Studies in Vayikra.* Israel: Haomanim Press, 1996.

Orwell, George. "Politics and the English Language" in *A Collection of Essays*. Garden City, New York: Anchor Books, 1954.

Shiloach, Amnon. *Jewish Musical Traditions*. Detroit, Michigan: Wayne State University Press: 1992.

Weisberg, David. "The Rare Accents of the Twenty-One Books" in *Jewish Quarterly Review*. Volume 56, 1966.

Wickes, Warren. *Two Treatises on the Accentuation of the Old Testament*. New York: Ktav, 1970. (Wickes' original work was published in 1887).

About the Author

Joshua Gettinger describes himself: "I am not a clergyman or a professional Judaic scholar. I have spent the last thirty years of my life enjoying the considerable satisfaction of practicing small town family medicine. I have delivered babies, helped people with illnesses and personal crises, and assisted patients and families at the time of death. I am fortunate to have a life partnership with an extraordinary woman who is full of energy and plans. Together we have raised four children in rural East Tennessee."

Dr. Gettinger and his wife, Dr. Barbara Levin, live in Madisonville, Tennessee, and belong to Heska Amuna Synagogue in Knoxville, Tennessee where he frequently reads Torah.

CPSIA information can be obtained at www.ICGtesting.com
Printed in the USA
BVOW031317091212

307690BV00001B/5/P

9 780981 679341